AUSTRIAN
Cooking and Baking

GRETEL BEER

DOVER PUBLICATIONS, INC.

New York

This Dover edition, first published in 1975, is an
unabridged and unaltered republication of the
work originally published under the title *Austrian
Cooking* in 1954 by Andre Deutsch.

International Standard Book Number
ISBN-13: 978-0-486-23220-1
ISBN-10: 0-486-23220-4

Manufactured in the United States by LSC COMMUNICATIONS
23220417   2020
www.doverpublications.com

TO
EVELYN FORBES

GRATEFUL ACKNOWLEDGEMENTS

... to all members of my family who, for generations, noted and collected recipes: in neat books, full of asides and family gossip; on scraps of paper now yellowed with age; thin and spidery handwritings and bold ones written in indelible pencil; recipes passed on by word of mouth, altered and amended as the years went on and memories weakened. Grateful thanks to all of them ... and to my husband who was never too surprised to test any samples that were going —no matter at what time of day or night they were proffered.

G. B.

CONTENTS

INTRODUCTION

*

THE culinary bouquet of Austria is made up of many fragrances. Of sugar and butter and rum. Of toasted almonds and chestnuts roasting at street corners. Of new wine and old love for recipes passed from mother to daughter. Of fresh coffee and comfortable gossip. Of sweet whipped cream and a leisurely contemplation of life. Of freshly scrubbed wooden tables and mounds of yeast dough rising in deep bowls. Of strong beer and Gulasch spiced with caraway seeds. But above all, of love for good food and the spirit of adventure that goes into its making.

The culinary flavour of Austria is a gentle flavour. It knows of the fiery spices of Hungary and the elegance of French cuisine. It derives much of its strength from Moravia and much of its daring from Poland. It is a broadminded flavour—if flavours can be broadminded—a flavour that knows the meaning of compromise. . . .

GRETEL BEER

CONVERSION TABLES FOR FOREIGN EQUIVALENTS

DRY INGREDIENTS

Ounces	Grams	Grams	Ounces	Pounds	Kilograms	Kilograms	Pounds
1 =	28.35	1 =	0.035	1 =	0.454	1 =	2.205
2	56.70	2	0.07	2	0.91	2	4.41
3	85.05	3	0.11	3	1.36	3	6.61
4	113.40	4	0.14	4	1.81	4	8.82
5	141.75	5	0.18	5	2.27	5	11.02
6	170.10	6	0.21	6	2.72	6	13.23
7	198.45	7	0.25	7	3.18	7	15.43
8	226.80	8	0.28	8	3.63	8	17.64
9	255.15	9	0.32	9	4.08	9	19.84
10	283.50	10	0.35	10	4.54	10	22.05
11	311.85	11	0.39	11	4.99	11	24.26
12	340.20	12	0.42	12	5.44	12	26.46
13	368.55	13	0.46	13	5.90	13	28.67
14	396.90	14	0.49	14	6.35	14	30.87
15	425.25	15	0.53	15	6.81	15	33.08
16	453.60	16	0.57				

LIQUID INGREDIENTS

Liquid Ounces	Milliliters	Milliliters	Liquid Ounces	Quarts	Liters	Liters	Quarts
1 =	29.573	1 =	0.034	1 =	0.946	1 =	1.057
2	59.15	2	0.07	2	1.89	2	2.11
3	88.72	3	0.10	3	2.84	3	3.17
4	118.30	4	0.14	4	3.79	4	4.23
5	147.87	5	0.17	5	4.73	5	5.28
6	177.44	6	0.20	6	5.68	6	6.34
7	207.02	7	0.24	7	6.62	7	7.40
8	236.59	8	0.27	8	7.57	8	8.45
9	266.16	9	0.30	9	8.52	9	9.51
10	295.73	10	0.33	10	9.47	10	10.57

Gallons (American)	Liters	Liters	Gallons (American)
1 =	3.785	1 =	0.264
2	7.57	2	0.53
3	11.36	3	0.79
4	15.14	4	1.06
5	18.93	5	1.32
6	22.71	6	1.59
7	26.50	7	1.85
8	30.28	8	2.11
9	34.07	9	2.38
10	37.86	10	2.74

I'D LIKE TO EXPLAIN

*

About flour: in Austria one differentiates between *glattes* and *griffiges* flour, a distinction unknown here. Use plain white flour throughout, unless otherwise stated, keep it dry and sift before use.

About sugar: most Austrian cake recipes etc. call for icing sugar. Castor sugar or granulated sugar can be used, but the mixture will be slightly coarser. If you have to use granulated or castor sugar where it is a question of creaming butter and sugar, add a drop of hot water towards the end of the creaming process. This is particularly important for all types of butter cream fillings, etc.

About butter: a great many Austrian recipes are based on butter and the very flavour it imparts to a dish. For that reason you will find the words 'butter or margarine' used only rarely in the book. Of course you can use margarine, though I personally would never substitute it for butter in any kind of cream filling and the like. If you do make cakes and pastries with margarine, spare enough butter for the cake tin—it makes a world of difference.

About brushing over pastry with egg or milk or melted butter: for small pastries an ordinary pastry brush is too heavy. In Austria long goose feathers—cleaned and tied into small bundles—are used. Worth remembering next time you buy a goose. Alternatively, use a small paint brush and keep the pastry brush for 'heavy' jobs.

About whisking egg whites: a pinch of icing sugar added when whisking them is as good as the proverbial and often quoted pinch of salt. Better, in fact, when making cakes.

About cream: this is an essential part of Austrian cookery and 'mock' cream will not do. At the time of writing, supplies of cream are plentiful—alternatively I simply syphon the top off my milk with an eye-dropper or a fountain pen filler or with a special gadget bought for 2s. You can collect quite a lot that way—and I do not take *all* the cream off my milk, always leaving about a quarter of an inch at the top. Thick sour milk or yoghourt can be used to replace sour cream in soups, sauces, stews and cakes.

About flavourings: steer clear of synthetic flavourings. A few drops of lemon or orange juice, or rum or real fruit syrup are no more expensive and infinitely better than all the synthetic flavourings in the world. And keep a vanilla pod with some of your icing sugar (referred to as vanilla sugar throughout the book).

About cream cheese: pour your sour milk into a bowl. When it is really thick hang it up in a cheesecloth or clean tea towel. The moisture will drip out gradually and you will be left with what is called *Topfen* in Austria. I have referred to it as cream cheese throughout the book and it is used for many recipes, mainly sweet ones.

About adding rum to pastries which are fried: this is essential, as it stops the pastry from absorbing too much fat while frying.

About horseradish: quite a number of recipes in this book call for it. It is a longish root which can be bought at most Soho greengrocers. Keep it in water and grate off as much as is required (having scraped it clean first). Grate rather coarsely. Incidentally, it will make you cry a little, like onions.

About fat: keep the various kinds of dripping well apart. Trim the fat off too-fat pork, cut it into cubes and render it down.

About tough meat: a mallet for beating meat is one of the most useful kitchen utensils and no Austrian housewife would dream of being without it. The back of a knife is acceptable as a substitute—mark the meat with a criss-cross pattern. And a sprinkling of lemon juice will also help to break down tough fibres.

About pre-heating of oven: should be done always. Essential for soufflés, cakes, and most pastries.

About the selection of recipes: the culinary repertoire of Austria is curiously proportioned. A strict sufficiency of necessities and a rich abundance of all that is sweet and slightly extravagant—facts which had to influence my choice of recipes for this book.

TABLE OF COMPARATIVE TEMPERATURES

Centre Oven Temperatures °F	Thermostat Setting
240°–260°	$\frac{1}{4}$
260°–280°	$\frac{1}{2}$
280°–300°	I
300°–320°	2
320°–340°	3
340°–360°	4
360°–380°	5
380°–400° } 400°–420°	6
420°–440°	7
440°–460°	8
460°–480°	9

SOUPS AND THEIR GARNISHES

*

IN Austria a line is drawn between *echte Suppen* ('real' soups based on stock made from fish or meat or at least bones) and *falsche Suppen* ('phoney' soups based mainly on vegetable stock with quite often a meat cube or two added). This distinction does not reflect on the quality of *falsche Suppen* which are usually very good. It is made simply to get one's sense of culinary values right from the start, and to impress once and for all the fundamental seriousness of stock. Stock may be made of many things: beef bones or veal bones or the water in which a piece of bacon was cooked. It may be made of *Bratensaft* (gravy minus the fat, plus any scrapings left in the baking dish after roasting some meat) or a small portion of left-over goulash. It can be vegetable stock or an honest beef-cube dissolved in hot water. But it should never come out of a stock-pot which has been kept simmering for days, adding bits of this and bits of that!

CLEAR BEEF BROTH
KLARE RINDSUPPE

The best clear beef broth is one which has had more than a nodding acquaintance with a piece of beef as well as with some beef bones. This is not an extravagance, because there is no kinder (and more economical) treatment for a tough piece of meat than to simmer it slowly, with plenty of vegetables, and thereby transform it into what is known in Austria as *gekochtes Rindfleisch*. (In restaurants it usually appears as *gekochtes Rindfleisch—fein garniert*, which is the boiled beef sliced, served with five or six different vegetables and usually also chive or dill sauce.) It really works both ways—you get plenty of good soup, tender, luscious meat (with no shrinkage in cooking) and all that with a minimum of trouble. No wonder the Austrians set such store by their *gekochtes Rindfleisch* that they even select the better cuts of meat for that purpose. Thus they will make their choice between *Hieferschwanzl* and *Tafelspitz*, classed as *Gustostueckl'n* in Austria (specially delectable cuts), as well as *Kruspelspitz*, *Kavalierspitz* and *Dicker Spitz*. . . . Alas and alack, we shall probably have to be satisfied with a shin of beef (commonly known in Austria as *Wadschunken*).

Before starting you will have to decide whether you want to make what is known as *weisse Rindsuppe* (white beef broth—though its colour is really golden yellow) or *braune Rindsuppe* (brown beef broth). For the latter vegetables *and* bones (this is important) must be browned first in a little fat. Any surplus fat must be poured away and only then are water and meat added. If you have only a small piece of meat it is better to aim at brown beef broth as the initial browning of bones and vegetables brings out a fuller flavour and you may also add a little meat extract towards the end of the cooking time.

Having thus made your decision, you begin by preparing your vegetables. For about one to one and a half pounds of meat you need about two carrots, one large onion, two leeks, a turnip, one or two tomatoes, a celeriac or a stick of celery (the stringy part), some parsley (including roots) and about one pound beef bones (chopped into convenient pieces), salt and a few peppercorns. A few sprigs of cauliflower may also be added. Wash and clean vegetables, cut onion into quarters, break tomatoes into halves. Scald bones and rinse in cold water. Wipe meat with a cloth wrung out in hot water. Put everything in a large saucepan, cover with about three to three and a half pints of water and bring to boil. Lower the flame immediately and simmer very slowly until meat is tender. This takes about two to three hours. If bones only are used, simmer a little longer. Do not let it boil and *do not remove* any scum which may rise to the top. If you have plenty of bones and want to preserve the full flavour of the meat you may prefer to add the meat only when the water has reached boiling point and then lower heat immediately. Personally I do not advocate this—I must admit that it improves the flavour of the meat, but this improvement is in my opinion slight and the loss of flavour as far as the soup is concerned infinitely greater. When the meat is tender, lift out carefully, keep hot (preferably over steam) with a little of the soup poured over. Strain soup, leave to cool a little, then remove excess fat.

Straining through a fine sieve or clean tea towel (previously wrung out in cold water) may suffice, but for really clear soup proceed as follows:

TO CLEAR SOUP

Have ready some crushed eggshells and one eggwhite. Whisk crushed eggshells (yes, it can be done) and eggwhite lightly with half a cup of white wine (or about half a cup of cold water and a little lemon juice) and a cup of the soup, then stir carefully into boiling strained soup. Lower heat immediately and leave over lowest possible flame for another fifteen minutes and you will find that all impurities have sunk to the bottom of the saucepan, together with the eggshells. Strain off soup carefully. (There is another way of clearing soup—and jelly too—which involves the use of fresh prime beef. We shall not go into that, however.)

In Austria all soups consisting of clear beef broth plus an addition such as noodles, etc., are named after that addition. Thus you will find *Schoeberlsuppe* (Clear beef broth with *Schoeberl*) or *Leberknoedelsuppe* (Clear beef broth with liver dumplings), etc. The recipes on the following seven pages are all for such additions and there is no hard and fast rule as to whether they should be used with white or brown broth. Some of these *Suppeneinlagen* (as they are called in Austria) are of course so simple that they require no recipe—a little semolina sprinkled into the soup, or rice, or barley. Then there are *Fritatten* which are ordinary pancakes (unsweetened of course) cut into thin strips and dropped into the hot soup just before serving. And then there is *Bouillon mit Ei* which I value above all others. I believe that it is the best tonic after a tiring (and trying) day, with the possible exception of *Fernet Branca* (which I swear cures most ills). To make *Bouillon mit Ei* (clear beef broth with egg) you need one egg (or egg yolk) per person as well as the clear beef broth. Slip an egg yolk (or egg) on each soup plate and then pour the hot soup over. That is all. The heat from the soup just sets the outer 'layer' of the egg and you stir it into the soup as you eat it.

Here, then, are a few more additions for your clear soup:

BACKERBSEN

1 *egg*	*Salt*
2 *tablespoons milk*	*Fat or oil for frying*
1½ *oz. flour*	

Prepare a batter with the above ingredients; the mixture should be of thick, running consistency. Have ready a pan of smoking hot fat, about three-quarters of an inch deep. Holding a ladle in one hand, pour the batter through a sieve with large holes (or a perforated spoon) into the hot fat. Fish out as soon as the little 'peas' are golden brown, place on blotting paper to drain and keep hot. Hand separately with clear *bouillon*.

There is another and more thrifty way of preparing these little 'peas'. When making *Strudel*, keep the pastry trimmings. Cut out tiny rounds (we always use a thimble) and drop into smoking hot fat. Fry until golden brown and serve as above.

BISCUIT SCHOEBERL

Schoeberl are a typically Austrian addition to clear *Bouillon*. They are usually baked in a special tin (*Schoeberlpfanne*), cut into squares when cold and re-heated in the oven just before serving. Any cake tin is of course quite satisfactory, though a square one is preferable, but the mixture should not be spread higher than about the thickness of a finger.

| 1 *egg* | 1 *oz. flour* | *Pinch salt* |

Separate egg yolk and whites. Whisk egg white with a pinch of salt until stiff, fold into lightly whisked yolk. Fold in flour. Spread on a buttered and floured baking tin, bake at Regulo 4 until golden brown (about fifteen minutes). Cool on a rack, cut into squares when cold and re-heat just before serving. Hand separately on a warmed plate or add to clear *Bouillon* just before serving.

SMALL BUTTER DUMPLINGS
BUTTERNOCKERL

| 2 *oz. butter* | 3 *oz. flour* |
| 1 *egg* | *Pinch salt* |

Cream butter, add egg and flour alternately. Salt to taste. Cover bowl and leave to stand for about fifteen to thirty minutes. Cut small balls with the help of a teaspoon and drop into boiling soup. As soon as mixture has been used up, lower flame and leave to simmer for about a quarter of an hour.

EINGETROPFTES

| 1 *egg* | *Pinch salt* |
| *About 2 oz. flour* | |

Mix flour, salt and egg to a smooth batter (exact amount of flour naturally depends on size of egg). Pour batter through a funnel into boiling soup. Leave to rise once, then remove soup from fire and serve straight away.

CHEESE SLICES
KAESESCHNITTEN

1 *tablespoon butter or margarine*
1 *scant tablespoon flour*
4 *tablespoons milk*
2 *tablespoons grated Parmesan or Cheddar cheese*
Rolls

2 *tablespoons grated Dutch cheese*
1 *egg*
Salt, pepper
Grated cheese for sprinkling over top

Melt butter or margarine, stir in flour. Cook gently, do not brown. Gradually add milk, salt and pepper. Remove from fire, stir in cheese and finally the egg. Cut rolls into slices the thickness of a finger and spread thickly with this mixture. Sprinkle with cheese. Brown quickly in very hot oven (Regulo 8) and hand separately with clear *Bouillon*.

The cheese mixture can be prepared beforehand and the slices just popped into the oven at the last minute.

LIVER DUMPLINGS
LEBERKNOEDEL

5 *oz. liver*
2 *rolls*
1 *oz. dripping, butter or margarine*
1 *egg*
Salt, pepper

2 *oz. breadcrumbs*
1 *tablespoon flour*
Salt, pepper
1 *small onion*
1 *tablespoon chopped parsley*

Soak rolls in water or milk, squeeze out moisture. Mince liver and rolls finely. Chop onion. Melt dripping (or butter or margarine), fry onion and parsley lightly. Remove pan from fire, stir in liver, add minced rolls, egg, flour, salt, pepper and breadcrumbs. Salt and pepper to taste. Leave for fifteen minutes. Form small balls—about one inch in diameter—and drop into boiling soup. Lower flame and simmer gently for fifteen to twenty minutes.

SMALL LIVER DUMPLINGS
LEBERNOCKERLN

5 oz. liver	*1 egg*
3 rolls	*4 tablespoons flour*
1 oz. dripping, butter or	*1 small onion*
margarine	*1 tablespoon chopped parsley*
Salt	

Soak rolls in water or milk, squeeze out moisture. Mince liver and rolls finely. Chop onion. Melt dripping (butter or margarine), fry onion and parsley lightly. Remove pan from fire, stir in liver, salt, add minced rolls, egg and flour. Salt and pepper to taste. Scoop out small balls with a teaspoon and drop into boiling soup. Lower flame and simmer gently for about fifteen minutes.

LEBERREIS

Prepare mixture for *Lebernockerln* as above. Holding a large-holed grater or perforated spoon in one hand, force mixture through the holes with the help of a palette knife, so that it drops into the boiling soup in the shape of small rice kernels. Cook for a few minutes only.

LUNGENSTRUDEL

Strudel *pastry (see page 151)*	*1 egg yolk*
using 6 oz. flour only	*1 oz. butter or margarine*
4 oz. lights	*Chopped parsley*
1 small onion	*Salt, pepper, caraway seeds*

Clean lights and cook in salt water. Chop onion and fry lightly in margarine, together with the chopped parsley. Salt, pepper and caraway seeds to taste. Add chopped lights, toss in hot margarine, then remove from fire and bind with the egg yolk. Pull out *Strudel* pastry as described on page 152. Spread filling over two-thirds of the pastry, roll up as for Swiss roll. Secure ends, then make indentations about two inches apart with the handle of a wooden cooking spoon. Cut into slices where marked and drop into boiling soup. Cook for about ten to fifteen minutes. Alternatively, roll complete *Strudel* in a well-buttered tea towel, twist ends and tie well, then cook in boiling soup for fifteen minutes. Remove towel, cut *Strudel* into convenient slices and serve in hot *Bouillon*.

Fleischstrudel is made in exactly the same way, using cooked meat instead of lights.

SMALL SEMOLINA DUMPLINGS
GRIESSNOCKERL

1 *tablespoon lard, butter or margarine*
1 *egg*

4 *tablespoons coarse semolina*
Pinch salt

Cream butter, margarine or lard, gradually add salt, semolina and egg. Leave for one hour. With the help of a teaspoon scoop out small balls and drop into boiling soup. Lower flame as soon as all the mixture has been used and simmer gently for about fifteen to twenty minutes.

SMALL MARROW DUMPLINGS
MARK KNOEDERL

3½ *oz. breadcrumbs*
¼ *pint milk*
3½ *oz. bone marrow*

1 *egg*
Salt, pepper
Chopped parsley

Crush bone marrow lightly, place in a bowl over steam to soften. It should melt, but not get really hot (in Austrian culinary language this is called *zerschleichen*). Moisten breadcrumbs with the milk, salt and pepper to taste. Add softened marrow, salt, pepper, chopped parsley and finally the egg. Work well together, adding a little more breadcrumbs if necessary. Leave for half an hour, form small dumplings and drop into boiling soup. Simmer for quarter of an hour.

REIBGERSTL

For this you can use the trimmings from *Strudel* pastry or any paste left after making noodles. Alternately, make a very firm paste with 1 egg, salt and about 3½ oz. flour. Pat into a round and leave to dry, then grate on a coarse grater. Dry in the oven on a baking sheet, then sprinkle into boiling soup and cook for a few minutes.

SCHLICK KRAPFEN

PASTE:
1 *egg*
1 *tablespoon butter*
5½ *oz. flour*
Salt

FILLING:
6 *oz. cooked meat*
1 *egg*
Salt, pepper
2 *oz. dripping*
1 *small onion*
1 *tablespoon parsley*

Sift flour and salt, make a little well in centre and drop in the egg. Cut butter into small pieces and mix everything to a soft paste, using a knife for the first stage of the mixing, then knead well. Divide paste into two parts, sprinkle with a little flour and leave for half an hour. In the meantime prepare filling by mincing the meat finely. Chop onion and fry in dripping, add parsley and minced meat. Salt and pepper to taste. Remove from fire, stir in egg. Roll out paste thinly, place small dabs of the filling within one inch of pastry edge, about two fingers apart. Brush round filling with egg white or milk, fold over edge. Cut into semi-circles with a pastry cutter. Repeat procedure until all the pastry has been used. Drop into boiling salt water and cook gently for about fifteen minutes. Drain and serve in clear *Bouillon*.

NOODLES FOR SOUP
SUPPENNUDELN

4 *oz. flour*   1 *egg*
Pinch salt   1 *tablespoon water*

For making noodles, *Strudel* pastry, etc., you should have a wooden pastry board. Sift flour and salt, make a small well in centre, drop in egg and water. Stir flour in with a knife, then knead well. Pat into a round, then roll out thinly. Leave to dry for about half an hour. Cut into strips, about three inches wide. Place strips on top of each other, cut into very thin strips. Leave to dry on the pastry board, then cook as and when required.

FLECKERL

Prepare dough as described for Noodles. Cut into strips about the width of a finger, then heap on top of each other. Cut into squares. Dry and use as above.

VEGETABLE SOUP
FRUEHLINGSSUPPE

This soup should be made with the freshest of young vegetables. Peas, young carrots, a small cauliflower broken into sprigs, beans and—if possible—one or two kohlrabi cut into small cubes. For three pints soup you need about one pound vegetables. Toss vegetables, which should be cut into cubes, etc., of similar size, in about two tablespoons butter for a few minutes. Cover with a lid and simmer for another five minutes, then pour on three pints clear beef broth (see page 16). Cook until vegetables are tender—no longer. Adjust seasoning and serve.

FISCHBEUSCHELSUPPE

1 *lb. roes*	*Dash vinegar*
Bayleaf	*2 tablespoons butter or*
3 *peppercorns*	*margarine*
1 *onion*	*2 tablespoons flour*
Thyme	*Pinch sugar*
Celery	*Salt*

Cook bayleaf, peppercorns, onion, thyme and celery in about two pints water for half an hour. Melt margarine, add skinned roes, cover with lid and simmer gently until roes are cooked. Lift out carefully, stir flour into melted butter or margarine and brown lightly. Gradually add strained vegetable stock, vinegar and a little sugar. Cut roes into cubes, add to soup and serve with fried *croutons*.

Although *Beuschel* usually refers to lights, in the case of *Fischbeuschel* it simply means hard roe. In Austria the most frequently used are roes of carp or pike.

GULASCH SUPPE

This is really a meal in itself, fully deserving a good portion of meat. You can 'stretch' the meat if need be, replacing part of the quantity by a pair of Frankfurter sausages, cut into slices.

3 *large onions*
Fat for frying
1 *tablespoon paprika*
1 *teaspoon salt*
Caraway seeds

½ *lb. beef (shin for*
   preference)
1 *tablespoon tomato purée*
3 *large potatoes*
Dash of vinegar

Cut beef into small cubes. Slice onion finely. Fry onion in fat until golden brown, add paprika, salt, caraway seeds and vinegar. Add meat, stir once, then add tomato purée. Continue stirring until nicely browned, then add water to cover. Simmer very slowly for twenty minutes, then add potatoes cut into small cubes. Simmer until potatoes are soft. Adjust seasoning, add a little more water if necessary.

A small quantity of left-over goulash (see page 47) may also be used for making Goulash Soup: Warm the goulash carefully, so that it does not burn, then add sufficient hot stock (or water and meat extract) to give the required quantity. Add some cubed potatoes and some sliced Frankfurter sausages and cook until potatoes are soft. Adjust seasoning.

CALF'S HEAD SOUP
KALBSKOPFSUPPE

¼ *calf's head*
3 *oz. mushrooms*
3 *oz. butter or margarine*
2 *oz. flour*
1 *tablespoon chopped parsley*

Salt, peppercorns
1 *onion*
1 *large carrot*
Bayleaf
A little lemon juice

Scald calf's head with boiling water, rinse with cold water. Set to cook with salt, a few peppercorns, onion, carrot and bayleaf, taking care that it should be completely covered with water while cooking. Cook until calf's head is soft. Clean and slice mushrooms. Melt butter or margarine, add sliced mushrooms and a little lemon juice. Simmer in covered saucepan until mushrooms are cooked. Dust with flour, stir, then gradually add the strained stock. Simmer for another five minutes, then add calf's head cut into strips and finely chopped parsley.

ERBSENPUREESUPPE

½ lb. split peas
Stock (see below)
1 large onion
2 carrots
2 rashers bacon
A little sugar

½ pint milk (as much 'top' as possible)
Bayleaʲ, thyme
1 tablespoon flour
Salt, pepper

The best stock to use is the water in which some ham or gammon has been cooked. In fact in Austria the boiling of a ham or a piece of smoked pork is almost invariably followed by split pea soup. Let the stock get cold, take off all the fat. If the bacon or the gammon was very salt, cook two large raw potatoes with the peas—to be thrown away before the soup is passed through the sieve. Soak peas overnight. Pour away the water in the morning. Cut the bacon into small cubes, slice the onion finely. Melt bacon in a thick saucepan, fry sliced onion in the fat until golden brown. Add the peas, carrot, salt (if necessary) or the potatoes, a little pepper, sugar, thyme, bay-leaf. Cover with stock and simmer very gently until the peas are soft, then pass everything through a sieve. Slake the flour with a little of the milk, add to hot soup and cook for another ten minutes. Adjust seasoning, add remainder of milk and simmer gently for ten minutes. Serve with fried *croutons*, or small pieces of sausage heated in the soup, or both. A small piece of butter stirred into the soup just before serving is a good thing.

CREAM OF LENTIL SOUP
LINSENPUREESUPPE

½ lb. brown lentils	Lemon juice
2 large potatoes	1 bayleaf
1 carrot	Thyme
1 onion	Pepper, salt
1 tablespoon flour	1½ pints water
1 heaped tablespoon butter, margarine or dripping	1 ham bone or bacon rinds

Wash lentils and soak overnight in cold water. Wash again, then drain on a sieve. Slice onion and carrot, toss in hot butter until lightly browned. Add lentils, stir, then dust with flour. Brown lightly, add water, salt, pepper, thyme, bayleaf, sliced potatoes and ham bone (or bacon rinds). Cook until lentils are quite soft (about two to two and a half hours). Remove bayleaf and ham bone, pass everything through a sieve. Return to stove, add a little lemon juice, adjust seasoning and serve with fried *croutons*. A little yoghourt stirred in just before serving (or two tablespoons top milk) greatly improves the flavour.

CREAM OF GAME SOUP
WILDPUREESUPPE

¾ lb. game (weighed without bones)	Salt, pepper, nutmeg
	1 bayleaf
6 oz. chestnuts	1 small onion
1 tablespoon butter or margarine	Parsley
	Dash brandy
1 tablespoon flour	1 carrot
A small knob butter	Small piece celery

Make an incision across top of chestnuts, cook in water until

soft. Remove skins and pass chestnuts through sieve while still
hot. Cut meat into convenient pieces. Melt butter or margarine, add sliced carrot, onion, celery and parsley. Toss in
margarine until very lightly browned. Add meat, stir and add
salt, pepper and nutmeg. Add bayleaf and chestnuts and sufficient water to prevent burning. Cover with a lid and simmer
until meat is soft. Remove onion and bayleaf, pass everything
through a sieve. Return to stove, add two and a half pints
water and simmer for another fifteen minutes. Slake flour with
a little water and add to hot soup. Cook for five more minutes,
adjust seasoning and stir in a knob of butter and the brandy
just before serving.

CARAWAY SOUP
KUEMMELSUPPE

3 oz. dripping or butter   Salt, pepper
3 oz. flour   Fried croutons
3 pints water   2 Maggi cubes
1 tablespoon caraway seeds

Melt dripping or butter. Stir in flour and fry until golden
brown. Add caraway seeds, salt and pepper to taste. Gradually
stir in water, add Maggi cubes and simmer for twenty to
twenty-five minutes. Hand fried *croutons* separately.

PANADLSUPPE

2 stale rolls   Salt, pepper
1½ pints clear stock (prefer-   1 egg yolk
    ably from veal bones)   ½ cup cream

Cut rolls into cubes and cook with the stock until rolls have
been completely absorbed by soup. Salt and pepper to taste.

Whisk egg yolk with milk, gradually pour on the hot soup, whisking all the time. Sprinkle with chives and serve at once. A small lump of butter added just before serving greatly improves the flavour.

POTATO SOUP
ERDAEPFELSUPPE

1 *large carrot*
Parsley
1 *small celeriac*
1 *clove garlic*
1 *tomato*
6 *large potatoes*

1 *onion*
Salt, pepper, marjoram
Fat for frying
1 *tablespoon flour*
2 *pints stock (beef or veal)*

Peel potatoes, cut into small cubes. Add to stock, together with crushed clove of garlic, sliced carrot, celeriac, parsley and tomato. Simmer until potatoes are very soft, then push everything through a sieve. Salt, pepper and marjoram to taste. Slice onion, brown in fat, dust with flour and stir. Add soup gradually, stir in a little more water if necessary. Simmer for another ten minutes before serving. Sprinkle with chopped parsley. Alternatively, cut two medium potatoes into cubes and cook in soup until soft but not 'mushy'.

SEMOLINA SOUP
GEROESTETE GRIESS SUPPE

2½ *pints stock*
2 *oz. coarse semolina*
1 *heaped tablespoon good*
   dripping or butter

Salt, pepper
Chopped chives

Melt dripping or butter, add semolina and brown lightly.

Gradually add stock and cook gently for about half an hour. Salt and pepper to taste. Serve sprinkled with chopped chives. There are numerous versions and improvements to this particular soup—sliced mushrooms may be added to the stock, or it can be bound with an egg yolk in the usual way just before serving. It is a good soup, a quick soup—and a friendly one!

CAULIFLOWER SOUP
KARFIOLSUPPE

1 *medium size cauliflower*	*Salt, pepper, nutmeg*
1 *egg yolk*	*Chopped parsley*
⅛ *pint milk*	2 *oz. butter or margarine*
3 *pints water or stock*	2 *oz. flour*

Cook cauliflower in salt water, being careful that it should not overcook. Lift out carefully, separate into small sprigs. Keep back a handful of sprigs, pass remainder through a sieve. Make a white roux with butter (or margarine) and flour, add water in which cauliflower has been cooked, cauliflower purée, salt, pepper and nutmeg. Simmer for a few minutes. Whisk egg yolk and milk, add hot soup gradually, return soup to stove, but do not boil. Add cauliflower sprigs, adjust seasoning and serve sprinkled with chopped parsley.

SAVOY CABBAGE SOUP
KOHLMINESTRASUPPE

3 *pints stock*	2 *oz. parmesan cheese*
1½ *lb. Savoy cabbage*	1 *onion*
5 *oz. bacon fat*	*Salt, pepper, marjoram*
4 *oz. rice*	

Cut bacon fat into cubes, melt over a low flame. Add chopped onion and fry until golden brown. Shred greens finely, scald with boiling water. Drain and add to onions together with stock. Salt, pepper and marjoram to taste. Add rice. Simmer until greens and rice are tender. Adjust seasoning. Serve with grated cheese.

Alternately, the shredded greens can be added to the fried onion (no scalding), remaining procedure as described above.

STOSS SUPPE

1½ *pints water*
1 *teaspoon caraway seeds*
¼ *pint sour milk*
¼ *pint sour cream*

Salt
2 *boiled potatoes cut into*
    cubes
1 *scant dessertspoon flour*

Cook caraway seeds in water, with salt added, for ten minutes. Slake flour with sour milk, add boiling water gradually, whisking all the time. Return to fire, bring to boil once, strain. Add sour cream carefully, heat, but do not boil. Serve with cooked, cubed potatoes—add a dash of vinegar or a few drops lemon juice if necessary.

TOMATO SOUP
PARADEIS SUPPE

2 *lb. tomatoes*
1 *onion*
2 *carrots*
Small piece celeriac
3 *oz. butter or margarine*
2 *oz. flour*

A little lemon juice
Sugar to taste
2 *oz. cooked rice*
Grated lemon rind
Bayleaf
Salt, pepper

Wash tomatoes, cut into halves. Scrape carrots, slice. Cut

onion finely. Melt butter or margarine, fry onion until golden brown. Sprinkle with flour, fry lightly. Add halved tomatoes, carrots, chopped celeriac, bayleaf, grated lemon rind, salt and pepper. Cover with water or stock (about two and a half pints) and simmer until vegetables are soft. Pass through sieve. Add sugar and lemon juice (do not be afraid of adding a generous amount of sugar—about three tablespoons—tomato soup should have a distinctly sweet flavour). Place rice in centre of soup bowl, pour hot soup over it and serve.

MUSHROOM SOUP
SCHWAMMERLSUPPE

½ lb. mushrooms
2 oz. butter
1 oz. flour
2½ pints water
1 small onion

1 tablespoon chopped parsley
Salt, pepper
A little lemon juice
⅛ pint cream

Clean and slice mushrooms. Chop onion. Fry onion in butter until transparent, add sliced muchrooms, parsley, lemon juice, salt and pepper. Cover with a lid and simmer until mushrooms are soft, adding a little water if necessary. When mushrooms are cooked, dust with flour, stir and gradually add the water. Cook for another twenty minutes, stir in cream five minutes before serving, taking care that soup should not boil after cream has been added.

FISH

*

LAKES and rivers in Austria yield a large variety of superb fish, the preparation of which is kept very simple. A respectable carp or trout is cooked *au bleu*—not really an Austrian recipe, but a way of cooking fish widely adopted throughout Austria. Or it is baked in the oven with lots of butter and possibly cream. In the case of larger fish, such as pike or carp, it is quite often sliced, floured, egged and breadcrumbed and then fried. Then there is also fish in aspic jelly with some regional variations.

Mention 'sea fish' to an Austrian housewife and watch her turn up her nose. In an emergency perhaps, and even then with reservations. The preliminaries alone would fill a book. Soak in milk. Wash in vinegar . . . the main reason being that Austria is really too far away from the sea so that when the fish arrives it is generally quite a bit past its first prime. All of which accounts for the absence of recipes concerning cod, haddock and the like—though most of the recipes given on the following pages are suitable for any type of white fish.

CARP IN ASPIC
GESULZTER KARPFEN

Wash, clean and scale a carp, cut it into pieces an inch wide. Cut one onion, two carrots, one celeriac into strips and cook them in salt water until tender. Strain liquid into another saucepan, set aside the cooked vegetables. Make up the liquid to two pints, add a few peppercorns, a bayleaf, salt, a little lemon juice, thyme and two tablespoons good wine vinegar and simmer for twenty minutes. Add the carp, including the head (having removed the gills, etc.) and simmer until the fish is cooked—about twelve to fifteen minutes. Lift out the fish carefully and arrange it in a deep dish, leaving a little space

35

between each slice, but arranging the slices graded so that the head is at one end and the tail at the other. Sprinkle the cooked vegetables round the fish and between the slices, adding a few chopped pickled cucumbers. Reduce stock in which the fish was cooked to half by cooking it briskly in an open pan, adjust the seasoning, adding a little more vinegar if necessary, then strain it over the fish. Leave to set.

My grandmother always cooked some potatoes in the stock which she would then slice and arrange round the fish, together with the other vegetables and sometimes she would also stir a handful of ground walnuts into the strained stock before pouring it over the fish.

EEL WITH PARSLEY
GEBRATENER AAL

Wash and skin an eel, cut it into slices and sprinkle it with salt. Leave for half an hour. Wipe the eel with a clean cloth, arrange the slices in a frying pan, sprinkle with pepper and finely chopped parsley and add half a tumbler of white wine. Simmer over medium flame, turning the eel slices from time to time until thoroughly cooked and browned on top. No fat is needed, the eel will provide its own. If it appears to cook too quickly, clamp a lid over the frying pan for a few minutes.

PIKE IN CREAM SAUCE
GESPICKTER HECHT

Wash, clean and scale a pike, make a few incisions down the back and stuff it with small slivers of anchovy. Sprinkle fish with a little pepper. Melt a piece of butter in a baking dish, turn over the fish in the melted butter so that it is well covered. Add a few broken-up tomatoes, a little lemon juice and a quarter pint sour cream or yoghourt. Bake the fish at Regulo 6, basting frequently. Sprinkle with breadcrumbs and return it to the oven for a few minutes to brown.

BAKED PIKE
GEBRATENER HECHT

Wash, clean and scale a pike. Cream three ounces butter with three finely scraped anchovies and spread thickly over the fish. Sprinkle the fish with breadcrumbs and put it in a baking dish. Bake at Regulo 5, basting frequently. Peeled and sliced potatoes can be put around the fish and baked at the same time, but they must be dotted with butter or margarine before the dish is put in the oven.

CARP IN PAPRIKA SAUCE (COLD)
GESULZTER PAPRIKAKARPFEN

Wash, clean and scale a carp and cut it into slices. Take the weight of the fish in onions and slice them very finely. Barely cover the onions with water and cook until tender, add two dessertspoons paprika, salt and stir. Add the fish and simmer gently, without stirring, until the fish is tender. Lift out the fish and arrange it on a platter. Sieve the sauce and pour it over the fish. Put in a cold place to set.

PIKE WITH ANCHOVY BUTTER
HECHT MIT SARDELLENBUTTER

Wash, clean and scale a pike. Make a few incisions down the back of the fish and stuff the slits with thin slivers of anchovy. Melt a lump of butter in a baking dish, add the pike and bake at Regulo 6, basting frequently. Set the fish on a serving dish and keep it warm. Pound two anchovies to a paste. Melt three ounces butter in a pan, add the pounded anchovies, stir and pour hot over the fish.

CARP WITH SOUR CREAM
KARPFEN MIT RAHM

Clean, wash and scale a carp, leaving it whole. Make several incisions down the back of the fish, sprinkle with salt and pepper. Butter a deep fireproof dish well, cover bottom with scraped and sliced new potatoes, dot with butter and sprinkle with salt and pepper. Pour about a quarter of a pint of sour cream over it and place the fish on top. Pour another quarter of a pint of sour cream over the fish, dot with butter. Bake at Regulo 4 for about half an hour, basting frequently, then increase the heat to Regulo 7, sprinkle with breadcrumbs, dot with a little more butter and return it to the oven to complete baking.

FISH IN MARINADE
MARINIERTE BRATFISCHE

Specially suitable for small fish such as herrings, etc. If larger fish is to be used, it must be cut into suitable pieces. Wash and clean fish, wipe dry. Sprinkle with salt, paprika and dust with flour. Brown quickly in hot oil on both sides and arrange the fish in a deep earthenware or heatproof glass dish. In the same oil fry a finely sliced onion and one or two sliced mushrooms. Sprinkle with chopped parsley and add two sliced tomatoes, stirring all the time. Now add a quarter of a pint of good wine vinegar and half a pint of water (or three-quarters of a pint of white wine), one bayleaf, a sprig of thyme, one clove, salt and pepper and, if you like garlic, a crushed clove of garlic. Simmer for ten minutes, then pour the marinade hot over the fish, which should be completely covered. Cover the dish with mus-

lin and leave to stand for two or three days. Serve sprinkled
with chopped parsley.

SCHWARZFISCH

Although this recipe was originally intended for carp and
similar river fish, any white fish, including cod and haddock,
may be used.

Clean the fish, and cut it into convenient pieces. Sprinkle
with salt. Clean and slice one celeriac, one lemon including the
rind and one large onion. Put celeriac, lemon and onion in a
saucepan, together with five lumps of sugar, five peppercorns,
a blade of mace and a piece of root ginger. Cover with three-
quarters of a pint of water and three-quarters of a pint of brown
ale and bring to boil. Reduce heat and simmer for twenty
minutes. Then add the fish and simmer until tender. Lift out
the fish and keep it warm. Add about six tablespoons grated
honeycake to the stock in which the fish was cooked, two tablespoons butter, two tablespoons dark plum jam or redcurrant
jelly, one tablespoon each of raisins and sultanas, one tablespoon blanched almonds cut into strips and a few walnuts.
Bring to boil and pour over the fish. Serve hot—and this is one
of the dishes which taste better every time they are warmed up!

MEAT, GAME AND POULTRY

*

VEAL RAGOUT
EINGEMACHTES KALBFLEISCH

¾ lb. veal
1 onion
2 carrots
1 celeriac or top part celery
Salt, pepper
4 oz. mushrooms
1½ oz. butter or margarine
1 oz. flour

Small knob butter
½ cup milk
1 egg yolk
½ packet quick-frozen peas
½ small cauliflower
A little lemon juice,
chopped parsley

Wash meat, cut into convenient pieces. Put in a saucepan, together with carrots, onion, celery and cauliflower divided into small sprigs. Cover with water, salt and pepper to taste. Simmer very gently until meat is tender. Remove onion and celery. Melt butter or margarine, add sliced mushrooms, cover with a lid and simmer until mushrooms are cooked. Lift out mushrooms and add to meat. Stir flour into melted butter, cook but do not brown. Gradually add stock from meat, stirring all the time. Add peas to meat and pour sauce over it. Slice carrot and return to meat. Simmer for another ten minutes. Stir egg yolk into milk, add to meat, stirring all the time and taking care that mixture should not boil. Just before serving add a small knob of butter and a little lemon juice. Sprinkle with chopped parsley.

ROAST KNUCKLE OF VEAL
GEBRATENE KALBSSTELZE

This is sold by weight in most restaurants. Sizes vary greatly and when your *Kalbsstelze* arrives, all nicely browned and glistening, it will usually bear a little label somewhere, proclaiming its weight. The best of them are larded before roasting, a little trouble well worth while.

2 *knuckles of veal*	1 *tablespoon dripping*
Strips of bacon fat	*Water or stock*
Salt, pepper	

Lard knuckles of veal neatly, sprinkle with salt and a little pepper. Melt dripping in a baking dish, toss meat in melted dripping, cover with a lid and roast in oven, adding a little water from time to time (Regulo 5). Remove lid towards end of roasting to brown meat. When the meat is tender and nicely browned, take it out of the tin and keep hot. Add a little water or stock to the juice in the baking dish, stir well and cook a little to reduce. Pour over meat and serve.

STUFFED BREAST OF VEAL
GEFUELLTE KALBSBRUST

2 *lb. breast of veal*	1 *small onion*
2–3 *rolls*	*Salt, pepper*
Milk	4 *oz. mushrooms*
1 *egg*	1 *heaped tablespoon butter*
Parsley	*or margarine*

Loosen rib bones, but do not remove them. Make an incision between meat and bones to form a pocket. Sprinkle meat with a little salt and pepper. Grate onion finely, clean and slice mushrooms. (Fewer mushrooms may be used or mushroom stalks only.) Melt butter or margarine in a frying pan, add grated onion and fry lightly. Throw in sliced mushrooms and chopped parsley and simmer until tender. Remove rind from rolls and soak them in a little milk, then squeeze out all the moisture and add rolls to mushrooms. Fry for about half a minute, mix well with a wooden spoon. Remove frying pan from fire, add the egg and salt and pepper to taste. Fill the meat 'pocket' with the stuffing, sew up opening. Place meat in a roasting tin, add a lump of butter, cover with a lid and roast slowly (Regulo 3). Add a little water or stock during the roasting and remove lid of roasting tin towards the end. Before serving take out the thread and slice meat downwards between the bones.

KALBSGULASCH

1 *lb. veal*	1 *tablespoon paprika*
½ *lb. onions*	¼ *pint sour cream*
Fat for frying	1 *tablespoon tomato purée*
Salt	1 *tablespoon flour*

Chop onions or cut them into rings. Fry onions in fat until golden brown, dust with paprika, stir, then add about two tablespoons water. Cut meat into cubes, dust with flour and add to onions. Fry lightly until water has evaporated. Add tomato purée, salt and cover with a lid. Simmer very gently until meat is tender, adding a little water as this becomes necessary. Finally stir in the sour cream, cook for a few more minutes and serve with *Nockerl* (page 90).

KALBSVOEGERL

There is more in a knuckle of veal than meets the eye. If you remove the bone (cutting right down to the bone first and shaving carefully all round it—I use a so-called 'map-knife' for this purpose, available at most good stationers) you will find that the meat falls into several oblong portions according to the fibres of the meat. Separate meat into these portions, lard them with strips of bacon fat and take your choice from several good ways of cooking them: you can roll up the meat (along the fibres, not across), tie it securely with cotton or thin string and simmer the meat gently with onions, tomatoes and a few small carrots. Or you can roast them in the oven with a little dripping (covered baking dish, please) and finish them off in a cream sauce. Or—most satisfying of all—you can spread any good stuffing over the meat, roll it up as before and roast or braise the meat according to your taste.

Incidentally, veal thus prepared is called *Voegerl* (little birds) because when rolled and tied it resembles a small bird trussed for roasting or braising.

VEAL ESCALLOPS
WIENER SCHNITZEL

Wiener Schnitzel is simple enough to prepare—if you have the meat, that is (and the meat in this case should be best fillet of veal). Everybody in Vienna will tell you that. Just a nice piece of veal dipped in egg and breadcrumbs and fried. *And* you should be able to slip a knife easily between the coating and the meat. *And* the coating should be golden brown—not dark brown. *And* any self-respecting *Schnitzel* should about cover your plate (after frying). *And* some wicked people smother it in gravy, for no reason at all. *And* others decorate it with slices of hard-boiled egg *and* an olive *and* bits of anchovy curled round, when all a *Wiener Schnitzel* really longs for is just a nice wedge of lemon—not a coyly crimped slice which is of no use to anyone. . . . As you will see from the following recipe, *Wiener Schnitzel* is, after all, just a nice piece of veal dipped in egg and breadcrumbs and fried. Here's how:

Trim veal escallops neatly, make a few incisions all round the edges. Beat escallops well. Have ready three soup plates: one with flour, one with egg mixed with a little cold milk and a pinch of salt, and a third one with good breadcrumbs (*not* toasted crumbs). Dip escallops first into flour, shake off surplus, then into the beaten egg and finally into the breadcrumbs. Do not press down the crumbs, just shake off surplus.

Do not keep escallops too long before frying. Fry escallops in deep smoking hot lard or oil. Do not fry too many escallops at the same time. Fry until golden brown on one side, turn carefully, fry other side. Drain escallops on crumpled kitchen paper and keep hot. That is all—you may even trim your *Wiener Schnitzel* with a little bit of pickled cucumber (the small, sharp kind) if you wish! Average weight of escallop (before coating with flour, etc.): about four ounces.

NATURSCHNITZEL

Trim escallops, make a few incisions around the edge and beat escallops well. Rub lightly with salt and pepper—some cooks also dust one side with a little flour. Melt some butter (or pure lard or good dripping) in a frying pan. Fry escallops on both sides (if the escallops have been floured, fry the floured side first), lift out and keep hot. Carefully pour off surplus fat, but see that all the little brown bits stay in the pan. Stir in a little stock, then add a good knob of butter. As soon as the mixture begins to bubble, pour over meat and serve at once.

RAHMSCHNITZEL

4 veal escallops	*Chopped capers*
A little flour	*Salt, pepper*
Butter for frying	*1 teaspoon French mustard*
½ cup cream	*Paprika*
½ cup water	*Lemon juice*

Trim escallops, then beat well to flatten. Rub lightly with salt, dust one side with flour. Fry escallops in butter, lift out carefully and keep hot. Pour a little water into frying pan, stir, then add chopped capers, pepper, paprika, French mustard. Bring to boil, then stir in cream and lemon juice. Adjust seasoning, add a little more water if necessary, stir and pour over meat. Serve at once.

PARISER SCHNITZEL

Trim veal escallops neatly, make a few incisions round the edges and beat well. Sprinkle them with a little salt and pepper, flour lightly, then dip into beaten egg to which about a tablespoon milk has been added. Fry escallops in smoking hot fat or oil until golden brown on both sides, drain well . . . and as our old cook would say, 'they are very popular with the gentlemen'. . . .

ESTERHAZY ROSTBRATEN

Trim small beefsteaks neatly, flatten with a mallet or a rolling pin. Sprinkle steaks with salt, pepper and paprika and a light dusting of flour. Cover bottom of a thick saucepan first with strips of bacon fat, then with an onion and a large carrot cut into strips. Add a bayleaf, a pinch of thyme and marjoram, a quartered tomato, a small celeriac and half a green pepper (both cut into strips). Sprinkle with salt, pepper and a teaspoon sugar. Cover with a lid and simmer gently (without stirring) until vegetables are softened a little, then remove the lid and brown vegetables without stirring, but adding a little water from time to time. (The temptation to 'give a good stir' is very great at that point—this you must not do, but you can shake the pan very lightly.) When the vegetables are nicely browned, add the steaks and toss lightly with the vegetables. Cover with a lid, simmer very gently until both meat and vegetables are tender, adding a little water if necessary. Arrange steaks on a hot dish, add a little sour cream to vegetables, stir well and pour over meat, having previously removed the bayleaf.

There is another version of the same dish where onions and carrots, etc., are cooked separately and only added to the meat before serving, but the recipe quoted above gives better gravy and juicier meat.

BOILED BEEF
GEKOCHTES RINDFLEISCH

See page 16 for *Klare Rindsuppe.*

MATROSENFLEISCH

Cut half to three-quarters of a pound of lean beef into strips, flattening each strip with the knife after cutting. Chop one large onion and fry until golden brown in about two tablespoons fat. Throw in the meat, add a pinch of marjoram, salt, pepper and cover with a lid. Simmer gently for five minutes, then add one scant tablespoon flour, a dash of vinegar and stir.

Continue simmering until meat is soft—about twenty minutes in all.

PAPRIKA BEEF
PAPRIKA ROSTBRATEN

4 *slices beef (fillet)*
½ *lb. onions*
2 *tablespoons fat*
1 *tablespoon flour*
1 *tablespoon paprika*

¼ *pint sour cream*
Salt, pepper
1½ *lb. potatoes*
1 *tablespoon tomato purée*

Trim beef, beat well and rub with salt and pepper. Melt fat, fry meat lightly on both sides. Lift out meat and put in a fireproof dish or casserole. Chop onions and fry in fat until brown. Add paprika, flour and tomato purée, stir in one cup water. Pour over meat and cover with lid. Simmer gently either on top of stove or in oven (Regulo 3-4). Slice potatoes and add to meat about three-quarters of an hour before serving. Stir in sour cream before serving, heat but do not let it boil. Adjust seasoning.

RINDSGULASCH

Gulyas is a Hungarian national dish. *Gulasch* is an Austrian national dish. There the similarity ends. What is known in Austria as *Gulasch* the Hungarians refer to as *Pörkölt*. After that things get really complicated. In Austria you can take your choice from *Rindsgulasch* (goulash made with beef), *Kalbsgulasch* (goulash made with veal), *Debracziner Gulasch*, *Znaimer Gulasch*, to quote but a few. The Hungarians say that there is no such thing as a *Gulyas* made with veal. Of course there is *Pörkölt* made with veal or *Paprikas* made with veal. . . . And as for *Debrecziner Gulasch* (Debreczin is a town in Hungary), they have never even heard of it. . . .

Anyhow, goulash is nice. All the year round. At all times of the day. In Vienna they talk lovingly of the good old days when a *Fruehstuecksgulasch* (Breakfast goulash) only cost a few *Kreuzer*. (In case this debauchery shocks you, 'breakfast' in this case means 'elevenses'.)

You get the best goulash in a restaurant. 'Freshly made', the waiter will assure you. 'How many days ago?' asks the prudent housewife, knowing full well that goulash tastes nicest when warmed up. . . . And as for the vitamins that get destroyed that way . . . well, anybody in Vienna will assure you that there is nothing like a good *Gulasch* to give you strength!

1½ *lb. beef*	*Fat for frying*
1½ *lb. onions*	*Salt*
1 *tablespoon paprika*	*Pinch marjoram, caraway*
1 *tablespoon tomato purée*	*seeds*
(optional)	*Vinegar*

Slice onions finely, cut beef into cubes. Fry onions in fat until golden brown. Add paprika and stir once, then add two table-spoons water. Throw in the meat, keep stirring until water has evaporated. Add tomato purée, salt, a dash of vinegar, mar-joram and caraway seeds and cover saucepan with a lid. Simmer *very gently* until meat is tender, adding water only in very small quantities as it becomes necessary. When the meat is soft, add a little more water, increase heat under saucepan, stir well and cook goulash for a few more minutes.

If you want more gravy, add a scant tablespoon flour slaked in a little water before final adding of water, stir and then proceed as described above, adding a bigger quantity of water.

There are of course a hundred and one ways that lead to a perfect goulash. A crushed clove of garlic may be added with the caraway seeds, etc., or a green or red pepper cut into strips. A friend of mine always adds a dash of strong black coffee, another one insists on a tablespoon of vinegar, and I remember being told once that a teaspoon of grated lemon rind really makes all the difference. . . .

Serve with *Nockerl*, or bread dumplings (see page 90), or with plain boiled potatoes (add a pinch of caraway seeds to the water while cooking).

SAUERBRATEN

Small joint beef	1 *teaspoon sugar*
¼ *pint wine vinegar*	1 *carrot*
¼ *pint water*	*Sour cream (about ¼ pint)*
1 *bayleaf*	*Salt, pepper*
2 *cloves*	1 *tablespoon fat or*
Thyme	*margarine*
2 *onions*	

Cut one onion into small pieces, put it in a saucepan with the vinegar and the water, bayleaf, cloves, thyme. Bring to boil and cook for fifteen to twenty minutes, remove from fire and cool. Put meat in an earthenware bowl, pour over the cold marinade, taking care that meat should be completely covered. Cover bowl with a cloth. Leave meat in marinade for at least four days, longer if possible, turning it over from time to time.

When required, take out the meat, fry with chopped onion, carrot and a little sugar. Add the strained marinade very gradually, as beef simmers in a covered casserole. Just before serving stir in sour cream, salt and pepper to taste.

WIENER ROSTBRATEN

Cut some beef steaks to the thickness of a finger. Trim off all fat, beat well. Make a few incisions round the edges. Sprinkle with a little lemonjuice, rub with salt, pepper and some paprika. Melt a tablespoon of good lard in a frying pan, throw in the steaks and fry quickly on both sides. Lower flame and add about two tablespoons of chopped onion. Continue frying at lower flame, lift out steaks as soon as they are cooked. (This is important as they will harden if left too long.) Keep steaks hot. Fry onions to a nice golden brown. Pour off surplus fat, add about one tablespoon butter, stir well and gradually add three-quarters of a cup of stock. Bring to boil, adjust seasoning and pour quickly over steaks. Serve at once.

WUERSTELBRATEN

I feel I ought to say here and now that this is, and always has been, my favourite way of cooking beef. That it is also an excellent way of making a small joint go almost twice as far, is merely coincidental. . . .

Take a lean joint of beef and trim off all fat. With the help of a skewer make four or five holes right through the joint, along the fibres of the meat. Push some Frankfurter sausages through the holes. If the sausages are longer than the joint, chop off at ends so that they do not protrude from joint. Fry one large chopped onion in a tablespoon fat, dust meat with salt, pepper and paprika and toss in hot fat with onion. Sprinkle with one tablespoon flour and fry for another minute. Transfer every-

thing to an ovenproof dish, swill out frying pan with one cup
water and pour over meat. Cover with a lid and cook gently
in oven until meat is tender (Regulo 3). Add a little more hot
water during cooking if necessary. Pass gravy through a sieve
before serving (it may be thickened with some yoghourt, but
this is purely optional). Serve meat sliced (across sausages, so
that each slice has some small rounds of sausage in it) with the
gravy poured over.

BRUCKFLEISCH

Bruckfleisch is the name for a collection of beef offal, consisting
of sweetbreads, liver, heart, milt plus a piece of *Kronfleisch*
which is a cheap cut of beef.

1 *lb.* Bruckfleisch (*see above*)	2 *tablespoons fat*
Small piece of celeriac or celery	*Pinch marjoram, thyme, caraway seeds*
2 *carrots*	1 *bayleaf*
1 *onion*	*Salt, pepper*
Parsley, including roots	1 *tablespoon breadcrumbs*
2 *tablespoons vinegar*	

Grate carrot, celeriac and onion. Chop parsley. Cut meat and
offal into smallish pieces. Fry vegetables light golden brown in
fat, add meat, etc., and toss in hot fat for a few minutes. Add
breadcrumbs, stir, then add vinegar and a little water. Add
bayleaf, thyme, marjoram, caraway seeds, salt and pepper.
Cover with a lid and simmer gently until all the meat is soft.
Remove bayleaf, adjust seasoning and serve with dumplings.

JUNGFERNBRATEN MIT RAHMSAUCE

Lard a lean piece of pork (suitable for roasting) with strips of bacon fat. Rub the meat with salt, pepper, paprika and sprinkle with caraway seeds. Cut a medium onion into rings and chop a few sticks of celery into small pieces. Also chop a little parsley, some parsley root and one or two carrots. Melt a tablespoon of dripping or lard in a frying pan, throw in the vegetables and brown them lightly. Transfer vegetables to a roasting tin, add the meat and very little water. Cover tin with a lid and cook meat slowly in oven, adding more water during the cooking. Remove lid of tin when meat is almost cooked. Take the meat out of the roasting tin, slice meat and keep hot. Add a small bottle of sour cream to vegetables, etc., in tin, stir well and strain over meat. The gravy may be thickened with a little flour, but this is generally not necessary. Garnish meat with capers and chopped parsley.

PORK WITH HORSERADISH
KRENFLEISCH

Usually this consists of part of a pig's head, one or two pig's trotters and a piece of pork belly. Chop meat into convenient pieces and place in a large saucepan. Add two onions, two carrots, a piece of celery, a few peppercorns, salt and a cupful of vinegar. Barely cover with water and simmer gently until meat is tender. Take out the meat and place it in a warmed soup bowl. Slice the carrots and add to meat. Reduce stock by cooking it uncovered for another five minutes. Strain some of the stock over meat and carrots, sprinkle thickly with grated horseradish. Serve with plain boiled potatoes.

ROAST PORK
SCHWEINSBRATEN

Rub meat with salt, pepper, French mustard, and a crushed clove of garlic. Sprinkle with caraway seeds. Place meat in a

baking dish, cover with a lid and roast in moderate oven
(Regulo 5). Baste frequently (a little water or stock may have
to be added). When the meat shows signs of getting tender,
remove lid of baking dish, make a few incisions in the fat right
down to the meat and finish baking without the lid. Place meat
on a hot platter, pour off surplus fat from baking tin. Pour a
little water or stock into baking tin, stir well and bring to boil.
Cook for a few moments, serve gravy separately.

PORK WITH SAUERKRAUT
KRAUTFLEISCH

¾ *lb. pork*
½ *lb. sauerkraut*
Salt, pepper, paprika
Caraway seeds

1 *clove garlic*
1 *small onion*
1 *dessertspoon fat*

Crush garlic under the blade of a knife with a little salt. Cut
onion into rings. Fry onion rings in melted fat until light
golden brown, add salt, pepper and paprika and stir. Throw
in the sauerkraut, the meat, previously cut into convenient
pieces and a little water. Add the garlic and the caraway seeds.
Simmer very gently until meat is cooked, adjust seasoning and
serve with potatoes or dumplings.

STYRIAN MUTTON STEW
STEIRISCHES SCHOPSERNES

1 *lb. mutton (weighed after all*
  bones have been removed)
1 *carrot*
Parsley and parsley root
1 *small celeriac*
1 *onion*

1 *dessertspoon fat*
Salt, peppercorns
Bayleaf, thyme
2 *tablespoons vinegar*
½ *lb. potatoes*

Cut meat into convenient pieces, pour some boiling water over meat and leave for ten minutes. Chop all the vegetables and fry lightly in fat. Pour away all surplus fat, add one and a half pints of water and bring to boil. Add meat, salt, peppercorns, bayleaf, thyme, vinegar. Simmer until meat is almost cooked, then add quartered potatoes and continue cooking until potatoes and meat are cooked.

Arrange meat and potatoes in a deep bowl and strain soup over them. Often served with a little horseradish grated over the top.

LIGHTS
BEUSCHEL

Use veal lights for preference.

1½ lb. *lights*	3 *oz. flour*
1 *onion*	1 *lemon*
2 *carrots*	*Sugar*
2 *tablespoons vinegar*	*Sour cream*
1 *bayleaf*	*Parsley*
1 *clove*	*A little French mustard*
A few peppercorns, salt	1 *dessertspoon chopped*
Parsley, celery	*capers* (*optional*)
2 *oz. fat*	2 *anchovies* (*optional*)

Wash lights well, place in a saucepan with onion, carrots, bayleaf, clove, peppercorns, salt, parsley, celery, a little grated lemon rind, vinegar and cover with water. Simmer until lights are cooked. Melt fat, stir in flour and prepare a brown roux. Add enough of the stock to make a thick sauce. Stir in finely chopped capers and anchovies, mustard, a pinch of sugar and a little lemon juice. Add lights cut into thin strips and just before serving stir in some sour cream. Serve with dumplings.

BRAINS IN EGG AND BREADCRUMBS
GEBACKENES HIRN

Use calf's brains for preference. Bring some water to which salt and a little vinegar have been added to the boil. Add the brains and poach for a few minutes. Drain and remove skins from brains.

Leave brains to cool and then slice them. Dip brains first into flour, then into egg to which salt and pepper have been added and finally into breadcrumbs. Fry in smoking hot fat or oil. Serve with salad or vegetables.

FRIED CALF'S HEAD
GEBACKENER KALBSKOPF

1 calf's head	½ lemon
½ onion	1 egg
2 peppercorns	Flour
Salt	Breadcrumbs
2 carrots	Pepper
Parsley	Fat or oil for frying
Celery	

Pour boiling water over calf's head, leave to stand for five minutes, rinse with cold water. Place calf's head in a large saucepan, together with onion, carrots, parsley, celery, half a lemon, two peppercorns and the salt. Cover with water and simmer very slowly until meat is soft. Lift out the calf's head and leave to cool. (The stock in which it was cooked can be used for soup or aspic.) Remove bones from flesh (this should be very easy and bones should come away without any effort). Cut meat into convenient pieces if necessary. Dip meat first into flour, then into seasoned egg and finally into breadcrumbs. Fry in smoking hot fat or oil. Serve with salad and Sauce Tartare.

FRIED CALF'S LIVER
GEBACKENE KALBSLEBER

½ lb. calf's liver   Milk
Flour   Breadcrumbs
1 egg   Fat or oil for frying
Salt

Cut liver into slices and soak them in milk for about one hour.
Dry carefully in a cloth. Dredge liver with flour, dip into
lightly beaten and salted egg and finally into breadcrumbs.
Shake off surplus crumbs. Fry liver in smoking hot fat or oil,
drain and serve with fresh green salad.

KIDNEYS WITH ONIONS
GEROESTETE NIEREN

Core and slice kidneys. Melt a large tablespoon good dripping
in a frying pan and brown a finely chopped onion in this.
Throw in the kidneys and fry, stirring constantly. When
kidneys are nicely browned, add one teaspoon flour, stir and
sprinkle with salt, pepper and a few caraway seeds. Gradually
add about half a cup of water and a dessertspoon vinegar.
Stir well and serve at once. Liver can be prepared in the same
way.

HIRNROULADE

½ lb. calf's brain   1 oz. flour
3 eggs   1 small onion
2½ oz. cooked potatoes   Parsley, salt, pepper
   (passed through a sieve)   1 dessertspoon butter
⅛ pint top milk

Wash brains well and remove skin. Melt butter and add the brains. Fry brains very gently (cover frying pan if necessary) together with the chopped onion. Remove pan from fire, add salt, pepper and parsley, finally stir in one egg. Separate yolks and whites of two eggs. Beat yolks lightly, add potatoes and cream well. Gradually add the milk. Whisk egg whites with a pinch of salt until stiff, fold beaten egg whites into yolks and potatoes. Fold in the flour. Line a Swiss Roll tin with buttered paper, sprinkle with a little flour. Spread mixture over this and bake in hot oven (Regulo 5) for about fifteen minutes. Remove paper at once, spread with brain filling and roll up as for Swiss Roll. Return roll to oven for about five minutes (Regulo 4). Slice roll and serve with green salad or vegetables.

ROAST MINCE
FASCHIERTER BRATEN

½ lb. beef	Salt, pepper, parsley
½ lb. pork	Fat
1 small onion	Flour
1 egg	Sour cream
2 rolls	

Remove rind from rolls and soak in milk or water. Mince meat finely. Squeeze out moisture from rolls and add to meat, together with salt, pepper, egg, chopped parsley and finely chopped onion previously fried in a little fat. Knead well and shape into a roll. Dust with flour. If possible lay strips of fat bacon or bacon fat on top. Melt a little fat or dripping in a baking dish, add the meat loaf, brush some of the melted fat over the meat, cover with a lid and roast in oven, removing bacon (or bacon fat) and lid towards the end to brown meat. Arrange meat on a heated dish, pour off surplus fat from baking dish and sprinkle in about one tablespoon flour. Stir well, gradually add enough water or stock to make a thick sauce and cook over low heat. Stir in a little sour cream and serve sauce separately. A few chopped capers may be added to the sauce.

TYROLEAN LIVER
TIROLER LEBER

1 lb. liver (calf's liver for preference)
Salt, pepper
2 oz. fat
Flour

1 small onion
⅛ pint sour cream or yoghourt
1 dessertspoon capers
1 dessertspoon vinegar

Slice liver and dust lightly with flour. Melt fat, and fry the liver. Take out liver and keep it hot. Fry chopped onion in the same fat, dust with a tablespoon flour and stir. Add salt, pepper, chopped capers, vinegar and sufficient water to make a thick sauce. Gradually add the sour cream (or yoghourt). Heat, but do not boil. Return liver to sauce, serve after three to four minutes. Rice is a good accompaniment, so are dumplings or *Nockerl* (page 90).

POTATO GOULASH
ERDAEPFELGULASCH

2 lb. potatoes
2 onions
1 teaspoon caraway seeds
Pinch marjoram

Salt, pepper, paprika
2 pairs Frankfurter sausages
1 tablespoon dripping
1 rasher bacon

Peel and slice potatoes (about the thickness of a pencil). Chop onions. Cut bacon into small squares. Melt fat, add bacon and fry lightly. Add onions and brown. Throw in potatoes, add salt, pepper, paprika and caraway seeds. Stir, then add just enough water (or stock) to cover, and the sausages cut into cubes or slices. Simmer gently until potatoes are cooked. A tablespoon or two of sour cream can be added just before serving.

STUFFED GREEN PEPPERS
GEFUELLTE PAPRIKA

4 *large green peppers*	TOMATO SAUCE:
½ *lb. lean mince (preferably*	1 *lb. tomatoes*
beef and pork mixed)	1 *small onion*
2 *oz. rice*	1 *tablespoon flour*
1 *dessertspoon fat*	1 *tablespoon fat*
1 *small onion*	*Sugar, a little lemon juice*
Chopped parsley	*Salt, pepper*
Salt, pepper	

Slice or quarter tomatoes, chop onion. Melt the fat in a thick saucepan, add onions and brown lightly. Throw in the tomatoes, salt, pepper and a little sugar to taste. Fry for a few minutes, then add the flour and stir. Cover with water, add a little lemon juice and simmer until tomatoes are pulpy.

Cut tops off peppers, remove inside parts and pour hot water over peppers. Leave for five minutes, drain off the water. Melt the fat, fry chopped onion lightly in the fat, add rice and fry until rice is transparent. Add three-quarters of a cup of water and simmer until water has been absorbed. The rice should then be half-cooked. Add the mince, parsley, salt and pepper. Mix everything together and fill peppers. Replace pepper tops and stand the peppers in a deep casserole.

Pass the tomatoes, etc., through a sieve. Mix together tomato purée and liquid and pour over peppers in casserole. (The tomato sauce should be fairly thin.) Cover casserole with a lid and either bake in oven (Regulo 3) or cook on top of stove over a very low flame until meat and peppers are cooked. Serve with rice or plain boiled potatoes.

G'ROESTL
(sometimes known as TIROLER G'ROESTL)

2 *tablespoons good dripping*	2 *cups cooked potatoes,*
1 *large onion*	*sliced or cubed*
2 *cups cooked beef,*	*Salt, pepper, caraway seeds*
sliced	*Chopped parsley*

Cut onion into rings. Melt half of the dripping in a frying pan, throw in onion rings and fry until golden brown. Lift out and keep hot. Add remaining fat, melt and throw in potatoes. Brown, then add meat. When meat and potatoes are nicely browned and crisp, return onions to frying pan, stir well, add salt, pepper and caraway seeds. Serve sprinkled with chopped parsley.

There is a very similar Swedish dish, called *Pytt i panna*, which is, however, usually topped with a fried egg per portion.

SADDLE OF HARE IN CREAM SAUCE
HASENBRATEN MIT RAHMSAUCE

1 *saddle of hare*	*Strips of bacon fat*
1 *cup red wine*	1 *onion*
Sour cream	1 *carrot*
4 *peppercorns*	*Fat for frying*
2 *bayleaves*	*Root ginger, thyme, marjoram*
A little flour	1 *tablespoon cranberry or red*
Salt	*currant jelly*
Bacon fat	1 *clove garlic*

Skin, trim and lard saddle of hare. Slice onions and carrots, put in a saucepan with peppercorns, bayleaves, thyme, root ginger, a clove of crushed garlic and marjoram. Cover with half a cup of water and simmer gently for five minutes. Add wine, heat, then remove from fire, pour over hare and leave for half a day. Take out hare, lard neatly with strips of bacon fat. Melt fat in a baking dish, add hare, cover with a lid and roast in oven (Regulo 5), adding marinade by the spoonful. When the meat is tender, slake sour cream with a teaspoon flour and add to sauce. Cook for another ten minutes, then strain sauce over saddle of hare before serving, adding red currant jelly to sauce just before straining.

LEG AND LOIN OF VENISON IN CREAM SAUCE
REHBRATEN MIT RAHMSAUCE

Skin the meat, then lard neatly. Rub the meat with salt, pepper, crushed juniper berries and a little nutmeg. Slice an onion, two carrots and a celeriac. Melt a tablespoon fat in a saucepan, brown onion and other vegetables lightly in the fat. Add the meat, brown a little on both sides, then transfer meat and vegetables to a casserole. Add a teaspoon French mustard, a bayleaf, a little thyme, two cloves and a little grated lemon rind, also about one cup water or good stock. Cover casserole with a lid and simmer in oven (Regulo 3–4) until meat is tender, adding a little more water during this time if necessary. Take out the meat, slice and keep hot on a platter. Add a quarter of a pint of red wine to the vegetables in the casserole, stir well, then add a quarter of a pint sour cream. Mix well together, heat and strain over the meat. Capers may also be added to the sauce. Serve with buttered noddles, or rice, and cranberries.

BACKHENDL

Clean and quarter poussins (quick-frozen poussins are excellent for this). Twist back the wings, make an incision on top of leg, twist back the legs. Dip chicken pieces first in flour, then in seasoned and lightly beaten egg, finally in bread-crumbs. Do not press down the crumbs, but shake off surplus. Clean chicken livers and stomach, also dip in flour, egg and breadcrumbs. Fry in smoking hot fat or oil until golden brown on both sides. Drain on crumpled kitchen paper and keep hot until all the chicken pieces have been fried. Serve with salad.

PAPRIKAHENDL

This is prepared in exactly the same way as Beef Goulash, using quartered chicken instead of the beef (see page 47). The chicken should be roasting chicken which is not quite as extravagant as it sounds (after all, simmering meat in gravy is always more economical than roasting it), but you can use a boiling fowl treated in the following way:

Clean but do not truss a boiling fowl. Put in a large sauce-pan together with an onion, two carrots, some celery tops, a little parsley, salt, pepper and the chicken giblets. Cover with water and simmer very gently for about one to one and a half hours, depending on size of chicken. After that time take out the chicken and cut into convenient portions (as a boiling fowl is usually much bigger than a roasting chicken you can get six to eight good portions that way). Melt a little fat in a saucepan and fry a large chopped onion until golden brown. Add a tablespoon paprika, stir once or twice, then pour in half a cup of water. Add the chicken, sprinkle with salt and pepper and stir well until chicken is nicely browned. Add a teaspoon of caraway seeds (optional) and a little of the stock in which chicken was cooked. Cover with a lid and simmer very gently, adding more stock from time to time as it becomes necessary. When chicken is soft, add a little more stock, in-crease heat under saucepan, stir well and cook for another few minutes. If more gravy is wanted you can thicken it with flour and add accordingly more stock.

The remaining stock in which the chicken was pre-cooked makes excellent soup and you can, of course, use only half the chicken for Paprika Chicken, cooking the other half in the soup or serving it in a number of other ways.

HAM ROLL
SCHINKENCREMEROULADE

4 oz. cooked sieved potatoes

3 eggs

Pinch salt

¼ pint milk (scant)

2 oz. flour

1 tablespoon chopped parsley

FILLING:

2 oz. butter

4 oz. ham

2 anchovies

French mustard, small gherkins

Separate egg yolks and whites. Beat together mashed potatoes and egg yolks. Add milk and a pinch of salt, chopped parsley. Beat very well. Fold in the stiffly beaten egg whites alternately with the flour. Spread mixture on a baking sheet lined with buttered paper. (Do not worry if the mixture seems too liquid, it stiffens considerably with the baking.) Bake at Regulo 5 until golden brown. Remove paper while still hot, roll carefully over kitchen paper sprinkled with flour and leave to cool.

Prepare the filling thus: Cream butter, add the finely chopped ham and the anchovies pounded to a paste. Beat in a little French mustard and some chopped gherkins. Instead of the pounded anchovies a little tomato purée may be used. Spread filling thickly over the cooled pastry, roll up again and cut into thick slices. Serve with a salad, or with vegetables.

SOME COLD DISHES

*

ASPIC JELLY
ASPIK

This forms a very essential part of the Austrian cuisine. The basic recipe quoted below can be varied according to supplies obtainable and alternate ingredients are given in brackets.

Into a large saucepan put one pig's trotter (or calf's foot), and a knuckle of veal (or one-quarter calf's head), all chopped into convenient pieces. If you have a chicken carcass, add this as well (or some of the giblets) and some ham and/or bacon rinds. Also add an onion, two large carrots, a celeriac (or some celery), parsley including some parsley root, one or two cloves, a few peppercorns, salt, a sliver of lemon peel, a bayleaf or two and some thyme. Personally, I also like to add a tomato broken in half and a few strips of green pepper. Add about four pints of water and a glass of white wine (or half a glass of good wine vinegar). Bring to boil, do not skim, but lower the heat and simmer gently for four to five hours, until the meat literally falls from the bone. Strain the liquid into a bowl and leave to set. When the jelly has set remove all fat—this must be done very thoroughly. Put the jelly in a saucepan and heat. In a bowl whisk together one egg white (turkey or goose eggs are excellent for this as they are so much larger than chicken eggs), the juice of a lemon, a small glass of white wine (or good wine vinegar) and a little of the melted, but not yet hot jelly. Also add the crushed eggshells and mix everything well with an eggwhisk (this sounds far more complicated than it really is). Bring remaining jelly to boil and stir in the egg white mixture very carefully. Bring to boil again without stirring, then lower the heat immediately. Cover saucepan with a lid and leave liquid over the smallest possible flame for fifteen minutes without any stirring. All the impurities will sink to the bottom. Strain the jelly through a clean cloth previously wrung out in cold water, taking great care not to stir up the sediment. If necessary, strain again through the cloth.

ASPIC JELLY AS GARNISH
Prepare aspic jelly as described above, and pour into wetted, shallow moulds to set. Turn out on to greaseproof paper and cut into cubes. Treated this way, aspic jelly is often used to surround cold meat—sometimes sprinkled with a little Marsala or Madeira. Alternately, the aspic jelly is chopped rather fine and piped over cold meats, etc., through a forcing bag.

TO LINE A MOULD WITH ASPIC JELLY
Melt the aspic over a low flame, remove from fire as soon as it has melted and stir until cold. The aspic jelly must be quite smooth. Rinse the mould in cold water and pour in the aspic jelly. Chill it well, if possible in a refrigerator, until sides of mould are covered with a thin layer of aspic. Carefully pour the still liquid aspic jelly back into the saucepan. Now you can decorate the mould with anything you may fancy—small rounds of gherkins, hard-boiled eggs, etc., dipping each piece into the liquid aspic jelly and standing your mould either on a bed of crushed ice or in a bowl filled with iced water. Chill mould again so that the decorations can set into the lining, then fill the mould as required.

STUFFED CHICKEN
GEFUELLTES HUHN

Clean a medium-sized roasting chicken. If you have it cleaned by the butcher, do remember to tell him not to truss the chicken for you, otherwise you will have holes in the skin, which is fatal. Cut the skin right down the back of the chicken, take off all the skin, being very careful not to tear it, and put it aside. Remove all the flesh from the bones (the carcass can be used for stock). Cut the white meat from the chicken breast into cubes, sprinkle with lemon juice and set aside. Weigh the remaining meat and add two-thirds of its weight in veal. Mince all the meat very finely, mince again or pass through a sieve. To the minced meat add salt, pepper, paprika, one tablespoon brandy, a few chopped black olives and two eggs. Work everything together until well blended, stir in two ounces of finely chopped bacon fat. Fold in the cubed white meat and, if possible, some cooked tongue, also cut into cubes. Stuff the chicken skin with this and, if you can, put one or two lightly fried chicken livers down the centre of the filling. Stuff chicken so that it almost takes back its previous form, sew up all the openings. Put the chicken in a roasting tin with a good lump of butter and brush it over with melted butter. Roast in a covered tin (Regulo 5), removing cover towards the end so that the chicken browns nicely. Leave to cool in the baking dish, cover with a board and weigh down a little. Brush with liquid aspic jelly and leave to set before serving. Serve sliced downwards—or whole, surrounded with tomatoes stuffed with vegetable mayonnaise—but on no account attempt to carve it! It must be sliced downwards.

BRAWN
HAUSSULZ

Into a large saucepan put a pig's trotter or a calf's foot, and half a calf's or pig's head, all chopped into convenient pieces. (Take out the brains beforehand and use separately.) Cover with about four pints of water, add a large onion, two carrots, two cloves, peppercorns, salt, some parsley including some root, a celeriac or a few pieces of celery, two bayleaves and half a cup of vinegar. Bring to boil, then simmer very slowly for about two and a half to three hours until the meat is quite soft. Strain liquid into a bowl and leave to cool. Take all the meat from the bones and chop very fine. In Austria it is usual to add some smoked tongue or pork, cut into small pieces, but failing that a little boiled gammon, cut into cubes, will do very nicely. Remove all fat from the cooled liquid, add liquid to meat and heat. Bring to boil once, then remove it from the fire. Leave to cool a little, stirring so as to keep it well mixed. When cool, add some chopped gherkins, capers and quartered or sliced hardboiled eggs. Taste the liquid when cold, add more seasoning and a little more vinegar—it should be quite sharp. Pour into a wetted mould and leave to set in a cold place. Turn out and serve cut into slices, sprinkled with finely chopped onion and a dressing of oil and vinegar.

If you possess a *Guglhupf* mould set the brawn in this—it looks rather nice. If you want to make a special effort, line the mould first with aspic jelly (see page 64) and decorate with slices of hardboiled egg and cucumber.

GALANTINE OF CHICKEN
HUEHNERGALANTINE

Clean a medium-sized roasting chicken, make a small incision on top of each leg, push back the skin and chop off the legs, leaving as much skin as possible. Treat wings in similar manner. Cut the chicken open down the back and bone it carefully, without tearing the skin. Put the chicken carcass in a large saucepan, together with the neck and stomach, a large onion, two carrots, peppercorns, salt, parsley and, if possible, a small knuckle of veal or a calf's foot. Cover with about three and a half pints of water and simmer gently for three hours. Meanwhile, spread out the boned chicken and beat lightly with a mallet. Rub the meat with salt, pepper and a tiny pinch of nutmeg and sprinkle it with lemon juice. Remove all meat from the chicken legs and the wings and mince finely. Also mince about half a pound of lean veal. Mix together the meat and mince again or pass through a sieve. Fry one or two chicken livers lightly in a little butter, set aside. Swill out the frying pan with one tablespoon water and add it to the minced meat. Add two egg whites and beat until smooth and quite firm. Beat in salt, pepper, paprika and about half a cup cream. Fold in two ounces bacon fat cut into cubes, four ounces diced cooked tongue or gammon, a few chopped black olives and—if available—some chopped pistachios. Spread half of the filling over the chicken, place the chicken livers down the centre. Cover with remaining filling. Fold together chicken and sew up all openings. (Do not try to coax it back into its original shape—it should simply be oblong.) Tie chicken into a clean napkin, secure ends well and put it into the strained, hot chicken stock. Bring stock to boil, lower heat and simmer for about three quarters of an hour from then onwards. Take chicken out of the stock, remove napkin and leave chicken and stock to cool a little. Tie chicken into another napkin and put back into cooled stock, weigh down a little and leave overnight. Take out the thread, brush over chicken with liquid aspic jelly and leave to set. Serve sliced downwards.

PATÉ OF CHICKEN LIVERS
HUEHNERLEBERPASTETE

The original recipe calls for goose liver which is almost impossible to buy in this country—unless you buy the goose with it! Chicken livers are much easier to obtain and, of course, there are quick-frozen chicken livers which are superb, if only one could get them more often. . . .

Clean one pound chicken livers, wash well. If using quick-frozen chicken livers, four packets are about equivalent to one pound, taking into consideration weight lost through waste if using the fresh kind. Melt some butter in a saucepan (unless there is some fat clinging to the livers which could be rendered), add the livers and fry them very gently, covering the saucepan with a lid. This takes only a few minutes and care must be taken not to overcook the livers, as this will harden them. Set aside a few particularly nice pieces of liver, push the remaining livers through a sieve while still warm. Swill out the frying pan with one tablespoon brandy and one tablespoon Madeira or Marsala and pour over the sieved chicken livers. Cream two tablespoons butter, add the chicken livers, salt, pepper, nutmeg to taste. Beat in half a cup of cream and about four tablespoons liquid aspic jelly. Cut the 'choice' pieces of liver into cubes and fold into the purée. Pile into a terrine, level top with a palette knife and cover with a thin layer of aspic jelly.

Alternately, you can line a mould with aspic jelly (see page 64), fill with the purée and put it in a cold place to set. Turn out and surround with cubes of aspic jelly.

KATZENJAMMER

Correctly translated, this might be described as 'the morning after the night before'. It is a noted cure for hang-overs of the milder type and, quite incidentally, an extremely pleasant dish for a light summer luncheon.

Cut some cooked beef into thin slivers or into cubes and cover with a marinade made of two parts oil, one part vinegar, salt, pepper and a little French mustard. Leave for two to three hours. Prepare the special mayonnaise described on page 82, seasoning it rather well. Lift the meat out of the marinade and fold into the mayonnaise. Also fold in some chopped gherkins and enough sliced potatoes to give a fairly loose consistency—on no account must the dish taste 'stodgy'. Sprinkle with paprika before serving.

HAM CORNETS
SCHINKENSTANITZL

Fry two chicken livers (or contents of half a packet of quick-

frozen chicken livers) lightly in butter. Do not let them overcook or they will harden—the whole process only takes about
three to four minutes. Take out the livers and push them
through a sieve. Swill out the frying pan with one tablespoon
Madeira (or Marsala) and one tablespoon brandy. Pour liquid
over sieved chicken livers. Mince half a pound of ham finely,
pass it through a sieve. Cream four ounces butter and beat
in the chicken livers and the ham, salt, pepper, nutmeg and
a little paprika to taste. Also beat in two to three tablespoons
liquid aspic jelly. Mix everything well and until quite smooth,
then put it to set in a cold place. Trim some lean slices
of ham into triangles. Put a dessertspoonful of the purée on
each triangle and roll into a cornet. Arrange the cornets on a
serving dish so that they rest on the folded part. Decorate the
open end with a slice of hard-boiled egg and brush over the
egg with liquid aspic jelly. Leave to set in a cold place.

LIPTAUER

This is all a question of taste—except for the proportions of
butter and cream cheese. Usually the amount of cream cheese
is twice that of the butter. The butter is creamed and the cheese
beaten in. After that you should add one or two finely scraped
anchovies, some capers, gherkins and a small onion, all very
finely chopped, also a pinch each of paprika, salt, pepper and
caraway seeds and French mustard. You simply have to taste it
(on a piece of bread) to see whether it suits your palate. Heap
the cheese on to a large plate, decorate it with a few dents made
with the back of a knife and sprinkle it with chopped chives—
that is all. Or you can serve your Liptauer 'restaurant wise',
that is to say, a small portion of cream cheese already mixed
with butter in the centre of each plate, sometimes shaped like a
large mushroom and dusted with paprika, surrounded by
minute portions of all the ingredients that go into its making—
and leave your guests to mix it to their liking.

VEGETABLES

*

WHEN the Austrians feel virtuous about their vitamins, they cook their vegetables in what they fondly believe to be the 'English' way. They do not feel virtuous very often and even then they compromise by sprinkling a plainly boiled vegetable liberally with breadcrumbs fried to a crisp brown in best butter. This applies particularly to cauliflower, French beans and Brussels sprouts, which are usually served as a separate dish when prepared this way.

From the fair-sized range of typically Austrian vegetable dishes I have picked a few which are little known in this country. Some of these, like the methods for savoy and red cabbage improve with each warming up. A dietitian's nightmare? I prefer to call it a good way to cook an otherwise rather dull vegetable.

BROWN LENTILS
BRAUNE LINSEN

Pick over one pound lentils, wash lentils, then cover them with cold water and leave to soak overnight. Pour away the water, put the lentils in a saucepan, together with an onion, a bayleaf, one or two carrots, a sliver of lemon peel, one tablespoon each of sugar and wine vinegar. A ham bone or even some bacon rinds tied together greatly improve the flavour. Cover with about one and a half pints water and simmer very slowly until lentils are tender. Dice about three ounces bacon fat, throw it into a frying pan and melt it down. Add a tablespoon flour, brown lightly and add it to the browned lentils. Simmer for another ten minutes. Remove onion, bayleaf and ham bone. Slice carrots into the lentils. Adjust the seasoning, adding more vinegar and sugar. Together with bread dumplings (see page 92) this is the traditional accompaniment to smoked pork.

PURÉE OF DRIED YELLOW PEAS
ERBSENPUREE

1 *lb. dried yellow peas*   2 *tablespoons butter*
Salt, pepper   *A few bacon rinds*
Parsley

Soak the peas overnight in cold water. Pour away the water,
put the peas in a saucepan, together with a small bunch of
parsley (including some parsley root if possible), some bacon
rinds, salt and pepper, and water to cover. Cook until peas are
quite soft. Drain, then pass peas through a sieve, adding a little
of the water in which they were cooked, to obtain a stiff, but
creamy consistency. Beat the butter into the hot purée and
serve.

RED OR WHITE CABBAGE
GEDUENSTETES KRAUT

1 *red or white cabbage*   *Caraway seeds*
   (weighing about 3 lb.)   *Salt, pepper*
2 *tablespoons sugar*   *Wine vinegar*
3 *tablespoons fat*   *Water or stock*
2 *tablespoons flour*

Trim cabbage, cut off stalks, etc., and shred finely. Wash
shredded cabbage well and sprinkle with salt. Fry the sugar in
the fat until golden brown, quickly throw in the cabbage
(stand away from the stove as it splutters a little). Toss the
cabbage in the saucepan, add caraway seeds, pepper, two
tablespoons vinegar and just enough stock or water to prevent
burning. Simmer slowly, adding a little more water as it becomes necessary. Slake flour in half a cup water and add
towards the end of the cooking time (not less than about ten
minutes before serving). Adjust seasoning—it should have a

distinctly sweet-sour flavour—adding more sugar or vinegar (or both). White wine can be used instead of water or stock and accordingly less vinegar. A grated apple is a good addition. Improves greatly with each warming up.

FRENCH BEANS IN CREAM SAUCE
GRUENE FISOLEN

1 *lb. French beans*	1 *heaped tablespoon butter*
1 *small onion*	*Juice of ½ lemon*
1 *heaped tablespoon chopped*	*⅛ pint sour cream*
fresh dill	*Salt, pepper, sugar*

String the beans, wash and cut into one-inch pieces. Throw into one cup boiling salted water, cover with a lid and cook until tender. Chop onion and fry lightly in the butter together with the chopped dill. Sprinkle with flour and gradually add the water in which the beans were cooked together with a little more water or stock to make a thick sauce. Add sugar, salt and pepper to taste. Add the beans and lemon juice and adjust the seasoning. Just before serving stir in the sour cream. Heat but do not boil.

CARROTS
KAROTTEN

1 *lb carrots*	*Chopped parsley*
1 *heaped tablespoon butter*	*Stock*
1 *dessertspoon flour*	*Salt, pepper*
1 *small onion*	

Wash and scrape carrots, cut into slices. Chop the onion very finely and fry in the fat together with the sugar, until golden brown. Add the carrots, salt and pepper and cover with about one cup stock. Simmer until carrots are tender. Add some more stock, heat and stir in the flour slaked in half a cup of water. Simmer for another ten minutes, sprinkle with chopped parsley and serve.

CARROTS WITH GREEN PEAS
KAROTTEN MIT GRUENEN ERBSEN

Proceed exactly as for the above, cooking a quarter of a pound of shelled peas with the carrots.

POTATO SLICES
ERDAEPFELSCHNITTEN

These are particularly good when served with game of any kind. Correctly they should be baked over a special mould so that they look like horseshoes, but the simpler shape does not alter the taste.

3½ oz. cooked sieved potatoes	1 egg yolk
3½ oz. butter or margarine	Grated parmesan cheese, egg
3½ oz. flour	or milk for brushing over
Salt	pastry

The sieved potatoes must be cold before work is commenced. Cut butter or margarine into small pieces, work to a smooth dough with the flour, salt, potatoes and the egg yolk. Cover with a cloth and leave for twenty minutes. Roll into a strip, fold sides to centre, fold over as for puff pastry. Cover and leave for half an hour. Roll out to one-eighth inch thickness and cut into strips. Set the strips on a buttered and floured baking sheet, brush with egg or milk and sprinkle with grated cheese. Bake at Regulo 6 until golden brown. Serve hot.

'G'ROESTE'

Cook some small potatoes in their skins. Peel and leave to
cool. Slice the potatoes or cut them into cubes. Melt about two
tablespoons butter or good dripping in a thick frying pan, add
the potatoes and fry them until nicely browned, stirring them
from time to time to prevent burning, but not stirring often
enough to reduce them to a pulp. Sprinkle with salt just before
serving.

COS LETTUCE WITH GREEN PEAS
KOCHSALAT MIT GRUENEN ERBSEN

1 *large cos lettuce*   1 *tablespoon butter*
1 *lb. peas (before shelling)*   1 *tablespoon flour*
1 *small onion*   *Chopped parsley*
Salt, pepper, sugar   *About ¼ pint milk*

Shell the peas, wash and shred the cos lettuce. Bring half a cup
of water to boil. Add salt, pepper and sugar and throw in
lettuce and peas. Cook until tender. Drain, retaining the
water. Melt the butter or margarine, add finely chopped onion
and fry until pale brown. Stir in the flour and brown lightly.
Add the water in which the vegetables were cooked and
gradually stir in a quarter of a pint of milk. Simmer for a few
minutes, until flour is cooked. Add vegetables, stir well and
serve.

MARROW
KUERBISKRAUT

Quarter a medium-sized marrow, remove seeds and peel. Shred
the marrow, sprinkle with salt and leave to stand for half
to three-quarters of an hour. Melt two tablespoons butter

or margarine, add half of a finely chopped small onion and brown lightly. Stir in two scant tablespoons flour, a little chopped parsley and dill, a pinch of paprika. Stir in sufficient water or stock to make a thick sauce, simmer for a few minutes until well blended. Squeeze out all moisture from the marrow and add to the roux. Add a scant quarter pint sour cream or yoghourt, a squeeze of lemon juice and a pinch of sugar. Cover with a lid and simmer for about half an hour.

RICE
REIS

The following two ways of cooking rice are the ones mainly favoured in Austria:

FIRST METHOD:

2 *cups rice*	1-2 *tablespoons butter*
3 *cups good clear stock*	*Salt*

Two tablespoons butter should really be used, one tablespoon only will do and there have been numerous occasions when I managed to get by with just a teaspoon of butter—but do not use margarine instead, it just doesn't work.

Wash the rice in hot water, dry on a sieve, shaking occasionally. Add butter to stock, salt to taste and bring to boil. Throw in the rice, let it boil up once, then lower the heat immediately. Simmer very gently in a covered saucepan until rice is tender.

SECOND METHOD:

2 *cups rice*	1 *medium onion*
2 *tablespoons butter or good*	*Salt, pepper*
dripping or oil	4 *cups water or stock*

Wash the rice in hot water, drain well. Heat the fat in a thick saucepan, add rice and finely chopped onion and stir over a low flame until the rice looks transparent. Add boiling water or stock, salt and pepper to taste. Cover with a lid and simmer very gently until rice is tender—about twenty minutes. Remove saucepan lid, put a clean napkin over saucepan to absorb any remaining moisture.

N.B. Using either method, the rice can be cooked in the oven instead of on top of the stove, Regulo mark 3-4.

RISI BISI

Fry two cups rice with a small finely chopped onion in two tablespoons fat until rice looks transparent. Add three cups boiling water, salt and pepper, cover with a lid and simmer rice very slowly. Hold one packet of quick-frozen peas under running cold tap to thaw, empty contents of packet into a bowl. When all the water has been absorbed by the rice, but rice is not quite tender, add the drained peas and simmer for another five minutes. Just before serving remove saucepan lid and place a clean napkin over the saucepan to absorb any remaining moisture.

SAVOY CABBAGE
KOHL

2 *lb. savoy cabbage*	4 *potatoes, parboiled*
1 *small onion*	*Parsley, salt, pepper*
4 *oz. bacon fat or 2 oz.*	1 *clove garlic*
butter	*Caraway seeds, marjoram*
2 *oz. flour*	*Stock*

Wash, shred and cook cabbage in very little salt water. Cut bacon fat into cubes, melt them in a saucepan and fry the chopped onion in the fat. Add the chopped parsley, the flour and stir. Gradually add enough stock to make a thick sauce.

Add the cooked savoy cabbage, the parboiled and cubed potatoes, salt, pepper and the clove of garlic crushed with salt under the blade of a knife. Simmer until potatoes are soft, adding a little more stock if necessary.

SAUERKRAUT

Wash the *Sauerkraut* in cold water. Taste a bit before cooking and also while it is cooking—it may be that the *Sauerkraut* is not quite sharp enough, in which case you will have to add a little vinegar.

For one pound of *Sauerkraut* slice a small onion finely and brown it in about two tablespoons rendered bacon fat. Add the *Sauerkraut*, salt, one teaspoon caraway seeds and a little pepper. Cover with water or stock and a dash of white wine (optional) and simmer gently. After half an hour, grate two medium potatoes into the *Sauerkraut* and continue to simmer it for another half to three-quarters of an hour. Adjust seasoning before serving.

MUSHROOM SOUFFLÉ
SCHWAMMERLSOUFFLEE

½ *lb. mushrooms*	1½ *oz. butter or margarine*
Salt, pepper	1 *oz. flour*
Butter for frying	½ *pint milk*
4 *eggs*	

Heat oven at Regulo 6. Prepare soufflé dish (butter it well and tie a strip of buttered paper round it to come about three inches over the top of the dish). Flour the soufflé dish lightly. Clean the mushrooms, slice them thinly. Fry mushrooms in butter, cover the frying pan with a lid and simmer the mushrooms until tender. Salt and pepper to taste.

Melt the butter, add flour and stir well. Gradually add the milk and cook mixture until it leaves sides of pan clean. Salt and pepper to taste. Remove from fire, stir until cooled a little. Beat in the egg yolks gradually, fold in stiffly beaten egg whites and finally the mushrooms. Pour into prepared soufflé dish and bake until well-risen and golden brown.

SALADS

*

Salads are many and varied in Austria. There is lettuce salad (quartered lettuce tossed in dressing, quite often decorated with quartered hard-boiled eggs), corn salad, cauliflower salad made with cooked cauliflower broken into sprigs, lentil salad—with bits of chopped bacon or ham and chopped onion, beetroot salad—sliced beetroot with a little grated horseradish and a sprinkling of caraway seeds, tomato salad—with chopped onion, parsley and chives. Salads made with slices of cooked celeriac or lightly cooked French beans and a delicious salad of crisp green peppers cut into rings. And then of course there is potato salad with plenty of freshly ground black pepper and chopped onion. In each case the dressing is an ordinary French salad dressing of two or three parts oil to one part of vinegar, with salt and pepper, a pinch of sugar and French mustard added, as the case may be. Theoretically . . .

In practice the proportions are quite often reversed and sometimes a little water is added to make the dressing less sharp. Or, probably remembering the original proportions of two or three parts oil to one part vinegar, the oil is partly or wholly replaced by water and just a drop of oil is added—as an afterthought. All this results in a tendency to have too much dressing so that the salad—this applies particularly to lettuce salad—literally floats in it. Sometimes quite a bit more sugar than is strictly necessary is added, and if the vinegar is then replaced by lemon juice (which is quite often the case), the whole thing is rather like lemonade. . . . Tackle someone about this aberration of taste and you will be given one of two answers: that a member of the household is on a strict diet, or that everybody likes it that way.

The situation is not utterly devoid of humour. Only quite recently an innocent visitor described one of these concoctions as 'wilted lettuce salad'—thinking that this was the effect intended!

79

The dressing may not be new to you, but perhaps you had never thought of making a salad with some of the vegetables quoted above and on the following pages. Incidentally, all vinegar used is wine vinegar—red or white.

CABBAGE SALAD (WARM)
WARMER KRAUTSALAT

Remove stalks, etc., from a white cabbage. Wash well and shred the cabbage finely. Cover with boiling water and leave to stand for half an hour. Mix a quarter of a pint of good wine vinegar with the same amount water, add salt, a little sugar and a teaspoon caraway seeds, heat. Drain the water off the cabbage, pour the vinegar, etc., over it when boiling. Leave to stand for a quarter of an hour, drain off moisture, heat and pour again over cabbage. Repeat until all the dressing has been soaked up by the cabbage (partly it will of course have been reduced through the heating). Cut some bacon fat into cubes, put them in a saucepan and render down the fat. Pour hot over the salad—including the small greaves.

CUCUMBER SALAD
GURKENSALAT

Slice a cucumber thinly. There is a cutter specially designed for this and similar jobs, called a 'Mandoline'. Sprinkle the sliced cucumber with salt, cover and leave for half an hour. Drain off all moisture by putting the cucumber in a clean cloth and squeezing lightly.

Rub a salad bowl with a cut clove of garlic, prepare a salad dressing consisting of three parts oil and one part vinegar, pepper, French mustard and a tiny pinch of sugar. Toss cucumber in the dressing, dust with paprika and sprinkle with chives.

CABBAGE SALAD
KRAUTSALAT

Remove stalks, etc., from a small red or white cabbage. Wash
well and shred cabbage very finely. Sprinkle with salt and
caraway seeds, put it in a bowl and pour boiling water over it.
Cover bowl and leave for half an hour. Prepare a salad dressing
with two parts oil, one part vinegar, pepper, sugar and a little
French mustard. Drain off all moisture from the shredded
cabbage, squeeze it lightly between the hands. Toss the
shredded cabbage in the dressing.

POTATO MAYONNAISE
MAYONNAISE SALAT

In Austria special potatoes called *Kipfler* ('shaped like a
croissant') are used for this, and more often than not the
mayonnaise is one prepared in the usual way—an egg yolk
mixed with a teaspoon vinegar, a pinch of salt and pepper, to
which about a quarter of a pint of good oil is added drop by
drop until the mayonnaise is thick. A little more vinegar (or
lemon juice) is then stirred in, together with about one teaspoon French mustard and the sliced and still slightly warm
potatoes (previously cooked in their skins and peeled) are
folded in. So far I have never managed to buy *Kipfler* in
England, but some of the potatoes which are imported from
the Channel Islands are very similar. Actually any small waxy
potato is quite suitable.

The special recipe for mayonnaise quoted below is particularly suitable for potato mayonnaise because it is fluffy rather
than thick and to a certain extent soaks into the potatoes. It is
equally good for a mayonnaise incorporating any other vegetable, fish, or meat, and in addition to this it is rather quickly
prepared and uses only a tablespoonful of oil.

1 *egg*	1 *teaspoon French mustard*
1 *egg yolk*	*Salt, pepper*
4 *tablespoons vinegar*	½ *teaspoon sugar*
2 *tablespoons water*	1 *tablespoon oil*

Place all ingredients, except the oil, in a bowl and whisk over steam until thick. Remove from fire, whisk in the oil, continue whisking until cooled. Fold in the sliced potatoes which should still be a little warm.

MUSHROOM SALAD
SCHWAMMERLSALAT

Clean and slice some mushrooms—field musrooms for preference—and throw them into boiling salt water. Cook for a few minutes only, drain well. Prepare an oil/vinegar dressing made of two parts oil and one part vinegar, salt and pepper to taste. Toss the mushrooms in this dressing while still hot, sprinkle a little finely chopped spring onion over the top before serving.

SAVOURY SAUCES

*

BOHNENSAUCE

This may sound rather unusual, but it is very good with boiled beef.

Soak a cupful white butter beans in cold water overnight. Pour away the water, put the beans in a saucepan, cover with water and cook until soft. Pass the beans through a sieve, then add two tablespoons oil, salt, pepper and vinegar or lemon juice to taste. Also add a small very finely chopped onion and/or some chopped chives. Blend very well and thin down a little with one or two tablespoons clear beef broth. Serve cold with boiled beef.

DILL SAUCE
DILLENSAUCE

Chop one small onion finely and fry in one tablespoon butter until pale golden brown. Add one dessertspoon each chopped parsley and chopped fresh dill and stir. Sprinkle with one tablespoon flour, stir and gradually add a quarter of a pint of clear beef broth, the juice of half a lemon, salt, pepper and a little sugar. Cook gently for ten minutes, stirring all the time. Add two tablespoons finely chopped fresh dill and a quarter of a pint sour cream. Heat very carefully, stirring all the time —do not bring to boil. Adjust seasoning, adding a little more sugar or lemon juice (or both) if necessary. Serve hot.

SAUCE MADE WITH HARD-BOILED EGG YOLKS

Pass the yolks of two hard-boiled eggs through a sieve and

mix to a smooth paste with a little French mustard, salt, pepper and vinegar. Gradually add sufficient oil to give the consistency of whipped cream, stirring all the time. Thin down with a little more vinegar, add about one tablespoon chopped chives and capers and blend well. Serve with cold meat—and if you can spare a tablespoon of good meat jelly, stir it in as well.

HORSERADISH WITH VINEGAR DRESSING
ESSIG KREN

3 tablespoons finely grated   1 tablespoon vinegar
  horseradish   Pinch sugar, salt, pepper
3 tablespoons oil   2 tablespoons stock

Heat the stock and pour it over the grated horseradish. Leave to cool. Mix together all the other ingredients, whisk well, then fold in the horseradish. Serve with hot or cold meat.

HORSERADISH SAUCE I
KRENSAUCE

Mix together four tablespoons cream, two tablespoons good wine vinegar, one teaspoon icing sugar and a pinch of salt. Stir in sufficient finely grated horseradish to give a thick and smooth consistency. Serve with cold meat.

HORSERADISH SAUCE II
MANDELKREN

¼ pint cream   1-2 heaped tablespoons
1 oz. ground blanched   horseradish
  almonds   Pinch icing sugar

Whip cream until stiff, add a pinch of sugar and whisk until smooth. Fold in the ground almonds and the grated horseradish (quantity varies according to strength of horseradish and taste). Chill before serving. Very good with cold meat.

This is not really a sauce and much nearer to a sort of savoury mousse. It can be frozen in the icecube tray of a refrigerator (previously set at maximum freezing point) and served cut into slices.

CAPER SAUCE
KAPERNSAUCE

2 *egg yolks*
2 *tablespoons olive oil*
2 *tablespoons wine vinegar*
2 *tablespoons water*

2–3 *lumps sugar*
Salt, pepper
1 *heaped tablespoon chopped capers*

Dissolve the sugar in the vinegar, add all other ingredients except the chopped capers. Whisk over steam until thick, remove from fire and whisk until cool, then fold in the chopped capers.

TOMATO SAUCE
PARADEIS SAUCE

1 *lb. tomatoes*
1 *small carrot*
1 *onion*
A *little chopped parsley, including some parsley root*

Thyme, 2 *cloves*
Sugar, lemon juice or vinegar
Salt, pepper
1 *tablespoon butter or margarine*
1 *tablespoon flour*

Wash the tomatoes, do not dry them. Put tomatoes in a thick saucepan with very little water, cover with a lid and simmer until soft. Meanwhile slice onion and carrots and fry until golden brown in the fat. Add the chopped parsley, thyme, flour, cloves, salt, pepper, sugar and a little lemon juice or vinegar. Add the tomatoes, including the liquid in which they were cooked. Simmer for ten minutes, then pass everything through a sieve. Serve hot.

CRANBERRY SAUCE
PREISELBEERSAUCE

As the name implies, this should be made with cranberries—cranberry jelly, to be exact. If this is not available, red currant jelly can be used.

Mix four tablespoons of the melted jelly with one dessertspoon rum, two tablespoons sherry, Madeira or Marsala and a little orange or lemon juice. Blend well and if you like the flavour of grated horseradish, add a small pinch of this. Otherwise stir in half a teaspoon French mustard—but on no account both. Nice with cold tongue, ham, game, in fact most cold meats—even corned beef.

ANCHOVY SAUCE I
SARDELLENSAUCE I

Rinse six boned anchovy fillets under cold running water. Shake a little to get rid of any water clinging to them, then chop them. Pound to a smooth paste with two heaped tablespoons butter. If no pestle and mortar are available, use a potato masher. Put the anchovy paste in a small bowl and stand it in hot water to melt, stir in the juice of half a lemon. Serve warm. Particularly favoured with pike or cooked pickled tongue. There is a short cut to the above recipe which does not quite produce the same result, but will do in an emergency: if there is no time to pound the anchovies, stir a dessertspoon of good anchovy paste (sold in tubes at most grocers) into the butter, then proceed as above.

ANCHOVY SAUCE II
SARDELLENSAUCE II

Fry one small finely chopped onion in one tablespoon butter.
Dust with one tablespoon flour, add six finely scraped anchovies
and stir. Add one large cup stock gradually and simmer for
about ten minutes. Just before serving stir in two tablespoons
cream. If you like your sauces sharp, add also a pinch of freshly
ground black pepper.

CHIVES SAUCE
SCHNITTLAUCH SAUCE

Mix together two eggs, a quarter teaspoon flour and one tablespoon water, stir well. Bring three-quarters of a gill of water to
boil, together with one dessertspoon sugar, one tablespoon
good wine vinegar and a pinch of salt and pepper. Pour the
water over the eggs, whisking all the time. Return the mixture
to the fire, cooking it in a double saucepan and stirring all the
time until thick. Add another tablespoon vinegar, stir well and
remove the sauce from the heat. Stir in two tablespoons good
olive oil and a heaped tablespoon chopped chives. Serve warm.

MUSHROOM SAUCE
SCHWAMMERLSAUCE

Served with dumplings, this makes a very satisfying main dish
—but it is equally good when it accompanies meat. Clean and
slice half a pound mushrooms (or even mushroom stalks).
Melt one heaped tablespoon butter, add the mushrooms, a
small pinch caraway seeds, salt, pepper, and the juice of half
a lemon. Sprinkle with chopped parsley and cover with a lid.
Simmer gently for about half an hour until mushrooms are
tender. Dust with one tablespoon flour, stir and add one ladleful

clear stock. Simmer for ten minutes, then stir in sufficient
sour cream to give thick, creamy consistency. Heat, but do not
let the sauce boil. Adjust seasoning and serve.

SAUCE FOR BOILED BEEF
WARME RINDFLEISCH SAUCE

When preparing boiled beef (see page 16), keep aside two
tablespoons of the clear beef broth and make the following
sauce to serve with the boiled beef:
    Cut three ounces butter into small pieces and put them in a
cup, stand the cup in hot water until the butter has softened.
In a bowl over steam whisk together two egg yolks, three tablespoons cream, the broth and the juice of half a lemon. Add
the softened butter gradually, whisking all the time. When
the sauce begins to thicken, serve at once—it must not
get really hot. A little salt may have to be added, but as a rule
the seasoning of the stock combined with the sharpness of the
lemon juice is all that is required.

ONION SAUCE
ZWIEBELSAUCE

Melt one tablespoon butter or good lard, throw in three
medium-sized onions cut into rings. Fry until pale golden
brown, then add a good pinch of sugar and stir well. Fry for
another minute or so, until onions are deep golden brown,
add a ladleful of clear stock or water, a pinch of paprika,
a dash of vinegar or lemon juice and a thick slice of brown
bread (without crust). Let it boil up once, then pass everything
through a sieve. Serve hot, either separately or poured over
sliced meat. Salt to taste.

DUMPLINGS AND THE LIKE

*

A *Knoedel* is a dumpling—sometimes large, sometimes small-ish. A *Knoederl* is a small dumpling, used mainly in soups (see page 21). A *Nockerl* is tiny to medium-sized, oval in shape and not really a dumpling at all. The only reason why I continuously refer to them as such is for want of a better name. Perhaps it would be more correct to call them *Gnocchi*, but that again would raise endless difficulties about *Gnocchi à la Romana* which are an entirely different thing altogether—so perhaps it's safer to stick to 'small dumplings'. There is a further point: in Austria *Nockerl* are made with the help of a *Nockerlbrett*, a thinnish piece of wood shaped in one with the handle. You hold it in your left hand and spread the paste over the wood. Small pieces of the paste are then cut off with a knife (dipped into hot water as you go along) and thrown straight into the boiling water or soup.

All very satisfactory—if you have a *Nockerlbrett*! Otherwise you will have to use the method prescribed on the following (and previous) pages of scooping out small balls with the help of a teaspoon—making the *Nockerl* look more and more like small dumplings. . . .

DUMPLINGS MADE WITH
BREADCRUMBS
BROESELKNOEDEL

¼ *lb. breadcrumbs*	1 *egg*
1 *dessertspoon flour*	1 *tablespoon butter or*
Salt	*margarine*
Nutmeg	

Cream butter or margarine, add the egg, salt and nutmeg. Beat in the breadcrumbs and the flour. Cover and leave to stand for half an hour. Form small dumplings and drop into boiling salt water. Cook for a few minutes only.

NOCKERL

Sift nine ounces of flour into a bowl. Dissolve one ounce butter or margarine in half a pint of milk, do not bring to boil. Remove from fire as soon as butter has dissolved, add one egg and whisk until well blended. Salt to taste. Stir milk, etc., into flour until a stiff paste is obtained. Bring a large pan of water to boil, add a pinch of salt and cut out small dumplings with the help of a teaspoon, dipping spoon frequently into the boiling water. Cook for about two minutes, then fish out one of the small dumplings and taste. They require between two and three minutes' cooking time—no more. Drain on a colander or sieve, rinse dumplings under cold tap.

Melt one heaped tablespoon butter or dripping in a frying pan, add the *Nockerln* and heat carefully, shaking the pan from time to time. The *Nockerln* must not brown. Prepared this way, the *Nockerln* are ready to be served as an accompaniment to goulash, etc. For *Eiernockerl*, break two or three eggs into a bowl, salt and pepper to taste, and whisk lightly. Pour eggs over the *Nockerln* in the frying,pan and stir with a fork, rather like scrambling eggs. When eggs have set, stir again with a fork and serve at once, accompanied by a fresh green salad.

MEAT DUMPLINGS
FLEISCHKNOEDEL

Prepare paste as for *Zillertaler Krapfen* (see page 94). Prepare a filling of equal quantities of finely ground pork and lean beef, a small chopped onion, pepper and salt. Bind with a little egg. Make small balls of the meat filling, wrap each ball with a thin cover of pastry. Drop dumplings into boiling hot salt water reduce heat and simmer for about twenty minutes. Drain, rinse with cold water and toss in hot fat to warm. Can be eaten with salad, *Sauerkraut*, in soup or in practically any other way.

SEMOLINA DUMPLINGS
GRIESSKNOEDEL

2½ oz. butter
1 tablespoon water
1 egg yolk

1 egg
Pinch salt
5 oz. coarse semolina

Cream butter, add the water gradually. Stir in the egg yolk and the lightly beaten egg together with three ounces semolina. Cover bowl and leave for quarter of an hour. Add remaining semolina, leave to stand for two hours. Scoop out small balls with a dessertspoon, handle very lightly and shape into dumplings. Drop into boiling salted water, cook until dumplings rise to the top. Drain, rinse under cold tap. Heat in sauce or gravy before serving.

SCHINKENFLECKERL

Traditionally, these are made with *Fleckerl* (see page 25) which should of course be home-made. Gastronomically, any good *pasta* is acceptable for this dish, provided it is small enough. This rules out *macaroni, spaghetti, canelloni* and the like, but *cornetti* (slightly curved, looking like broken-up *macaroni* and often erroneously sold as such), broad noodles and most of the *pastina minestrone* family sold in good Soho shops (bows, rosettes, etc.) can be used. It is difficult to give exact quantities as this depends entirely on the *pasta*, but the recipe quoted below is for about half a pound of *pasta*. Cook the *pasta* in rapidly boiling salt water, being careful not to overcook it. Drain and rinse under cold tap. Butter a deep ovenproof dish. Cream one heaped tablespoon butter, beat in two egg yolks and gradually add three-eighths of a pint of sour cream and a quarter of a pound chopped ham. Fold in two stiffly beaten egg whites and the drained *pasta*. Bake in the buttered casserole (Regulo 5) until nicely browned on top. Serve with a green salad.

Again, as with most traditional recipes, there are numerous variations. You can just toss the cooked *pasta* in a little hot butter and leave out the 'creaming of butter', simply whisking together the sour cream and the egg yolks. The whipped egg whites which are added at the end are also optional—leaving them out, however, gives a far less fluffy consistency.

HIRNPOFESEN

Blanch a calf's brain, drain and remove the skin. Fry a small, finely chopped onion in a little fat until pale golden brown, add the brains, some chopped parsley, salt and pepper. Stir over low flame until the brains are cooked, add an egg and, still stirring, remove the pan from fire. Cut a few thin slices of bread, using a French loaf if possible. Cut off the crusts. Dip the bread slices into milk for a second, then sandwich two and two together with the brain mixture. Press down a little and leave for about ten minutes. Dip into seasoned lightly beaten egg, then into breadcrumbs and fry golden brown on both sides. Serve with creamed spinach.

BREAD DUMPLINGS
SEMMELKNOEDEL

4 *rolls*	*Chopped parsley*
1 *egg or* 1 *egg yolk*	*Fat*
2–3 *rashers bacon*	*Flour*
(optional)	*Salt, pepper*

Use day-old rolls or an equivalent quantity of bread. Dice bread or rolls, chop the bacon. Fry the bacon lightly, add a little fat and brown the diced rolls in this. Break egg into a cup and fill up cup with milk. Mix milk and egg, add a pinch of salt and pepper. Empty contents of frying pan into a bowl and pour over milk, etc., while diced bread is still warm. Stir in four heaped tablespoons flour and leave to stand for half an hour. Form dumplings, adding a little more flour if necessary, and drop into boiling salt water. Cook for ten to fifteen minutes. Good with goulash, *Sauerkraut* or brown lentils.

Left-over dumplings can be used up in the following way. Slice the cold dumplings thinly and fry them in a little fat. Pour over one or two lightly beaten eggs and treat as for scrambled eggs. Serve with a green salad. This is known simply as *Knoedel mit Ei* (dumplings with egg) and makes a very popular light luncheon dish.

SERVIETTENKNOEDEL

½ *lb. cream cheese* 2 *eggs*
2 *oz. semolina* *Pinch salt, sugar*
1½ *oz. butter*

Separate egg yolks and whites. Cream butter with a pinch of salt and sugar, add egg yolks and semolina. Leave to stand for two hours. Fold in stiffly beaten egg whites alternately with cream cheese. Form one large dumpling and place it in the centre of a napkin previously wrung out in cold water. Tie ends loosely over the dumpling. Have ready a pan of boiling water to which a pinch of salt has been added. Slot the handle of a wooden cooking spoon through the tied napkin ends and thus hang the dumpling into boiling water—resting the wooden handle on the saucepan rim. Cover saucepan with a lid and ower heat. Simmer the dumpling for half an hour. (Hanging the dumpling into the boiling water in the manner described above prevents it from sinking to the bottom of the pan and burning.)

This dumpling, sliced and sometimes sprinkled with bread-crumbs fried in butter, is served with meat instead of potatoes. Sliced and sprinkled with melted butter and sugar, it is served as a dessert, usually accompanied by stewed fruit.

FRIED MEAT TURNOVERS
ZILLERTALER KRAPFEN

Sift half a pound of flour onto a pastryboard, add an egg (or egg yolk), salt and enough warm water to make a stiff paste. Knead well. Shape into a roll and cut off small pieces—about one inch long. Roll out each piece as thinly as possible. Prepare filling as follows: Cook one pound potatoes in their skins, peel and sieve while still hot. Add half a pound cream cheese, a quarter of a pint top milk, salt, pepper, one egg yolk, chopped chives or parsley and about three ounces finely chopped ham or greaves. Stir in about one dessertspoon flour to make a stiff paste. (More flour may be required, depending on the con-sistency of potatoes and cream cheese.) Put a good dab of this filling in centre of each pastry round, brush round filling with a little egg or milk, fold over and press together edges. Fry in smoking hot deep fat.

DESSERTS—HOT AND COLD
INCLUDING SWEET SAUCES

*

APPLE SNOW
APFELSCHNEE

2 large or 3 medium cooking apples	4 tablespoons sugar
	1 tumblerful white wine
1 tablespoon lemon juice	1 teaspoon Maraschino
3 eggs	Sugar to taste

Separate egg yolks and whites. Wipe the apples and bake them in the oven until soft (Regulo 4). Remove skin while still hot, mash the pulp and throw away the pips, etc. Put six tablespoons of this apple purée (about the result of the quantity of apples given), four tablespoons sugar, the lemon juice and the egg whites into a bowl and whisk over steam until thick. Using a rotary eggwhisk, this takes between five and seven minutes. Remove from fire and add one teaspoon Maraschino. Continue whisking until cool. Cover the bowl and chill—if possible in a refrigerator. Before serving, arrange the apple foam in a glass dish and serve very cold, with the following hot sauce handed separately:

Put the egg yolks, wine and sugar to taste (about three tablespoons) in a bowl and whisk over steam until thick. Serve at once.

BAKED PANCAKES WITH
VANILLA CREAM
CREMEPALATSCHINKEN

Prepare some pancakes as described on page 103. Sprinkle each pancake with grated walnuts and sugar and roll them up separately. Arrange pancakes side by side in a rectangular or oblong fireproof dish. Cook half a pint of milk with two egg yolks and about two tablespoons vanilla sugar in a double boiler until thick, pour over pancakes and bake in a medium hot oven until lightly browned.

PUDDING MADE WITH SPONGE FINGERS AND WINE
BISKOTTEN AUFLAUF

½ pint white wine
7 oz. sugar
Juice of 1 lemon
Jam

½ pint milk
About 20 sponge fingers
2 eggs

Butter a deep pie-dish. Put the wine and the lemon juice in a saucepan, add five ounces sugar and stir over low flame until all the sugar has dissolved. Dip each sponge finger into the wine, arrange sponge fingers in layers in the pie-dish, putting small blobs of jam between each layer. Whisk the eggs lightly with the remaining sugar and a little cold milk, heat remaining milk and pour over the eggs. Whisk well, pour over sponge fingers in pie-dish and bake until golden brown (Regulo 5).

CREAM PUDDING
CREME PUDDING

Whisk together half a pint of milk with a vanilla pod, three egg yolks, one dessertspoon flour and three ounces sugar over steam until fluffy. Butter a deep pie-dish and pour in a half-inch layer of this cream, having first removed the vanilla pod. Cut some sponge cakes into slices, sprinkle with rum and sandwich two and two together with jam. Arrange the sponge slices in layers in the pie-dish, covering each layer with a little of the cream, finishing with a layer of the cream. Bake at

Regulo 5 for ten minutes. Meanwhile whisk the three egg whites until thick, whisk in two tablespoons caster sugar, then fold in three tablespoons caster sugar. Heap the whisked egg whites on top of the pudding and return it to the oven at Regulo ½ until meringue has set. Can be eaten hot or cold.

GEBACKENE MAEUSE

7 *oz. flour*	I *oz. raisins*
I *large or* 2 *small eggs*	I *tablespoon rum*
2 *oz. butter or margarine*	¼ *pint milk*
½ *oz. sugar*	*Deep fat for frying*
⅓ *oz. yeast*	

Separate egg yolks and whites. Wash and dry the raisins. Cream yeast with sugar, add a teaspoon of the flour and a little of the milk (tepid). Leave to prove in a warm place. Sift remaining flour into a bowl, make a well in the centre, drop in the egg yolk (or egg yolks), stir in the yeast, melted butter and remaining milk. Add the rum and mix well. Cover bowl with a cloth and leave to rise in a warm place. When the dough has risen to about twice the original size, fold in the stiffly beaten egg whites and the raisins. Drop tablespoonfuls into smoking hot deep fat, cover frying pan with a lid and fry until golden brown on one side. Turn over and fry other side (without a lid on the frying pan). Drain on paper, dust with sugar and serve hot with fruit syrup.

GEBACKENES STROH

Make a smooth dough with three-quarters of a cup of flour, a pinch of salt, one tablespoon butter, one egg and, if necessary, a little milk. Knead well, then roll out as thinly as possible. Cut into noodles and drop into smoking hot fat. Fry until golden brown, drain on kitchen paper. Whisk half a pint of milk with two egg yolks and two tablespoons sugar over steam until thick. Arrange fried noodles in a deep pie-dish, sprinkle with one or two tablespoons washed and dried raisins and pour the egg cream over it. Brown in hot oven for a few minutes.

SEMOLINA CAKE SERVED AS SWEET
GRIESSTORTE ALS MEHLSPEISE

2½ oz. sugar   2 oz. ground almonds
2 eggs   1 oz. semolina

SAUCE *as for almond pudding* (*see page* 120)

Butter and flour a cake tin. Separate egg yolks and whites. Whisk together sugar and egg yolks, fold in the ground almonds, stiffly beaten egg whites and the semolina—in that order. Pour mixture into cake tin and bake at Regulo 4 for about thirty minutes. Leave for a few minutes in the tin, then tip cake carefully into a dish. Pour the sauce over it and serve warm but not hot.

KALTER REIS

It takes not a little bravery to quote a recipe which calls for half a pint of cream and which, translated, means simply 'cold rice': both facts are enough to frighten anyone. In fact only a truly wonderful dish like this could manage to remain known under such a terrible name.

Wash three ounces of rice and cook it in half a pint of milk with a vanilla pod and two ounces sugar until soft, but not mushy. While still hot stir in one-third of an ounce of gelatine previously softened in a little water. Leave to cool and, just as the mixture begins to set, remove the vanilla pod and fold in half a pint of whipped cream (a little less may be used). Arrange

in a mould rinsed in cold water and chill thoroughly. Turn out
on to a dish, surround with lightly stewed or quick-frozen fruit
(strawberries or raspberries) and pour over it a little raspberry
syrup.

KANARIENMILCH

A sweet sauce served with a number of puddings, etc.

1 *egg yolk*	*Vanilla pod*
½ *pint milk*	1 *oz. sugar*

Heat the milk with the vanilla pod. Whisk together sugar and
egg yolk, gradually add the warmed but not hot milk. Whisk
over steam until very frothy. Use as required.

DAMPFNUDELN

2 *oz. melted butter or margarine*	*About* ⅛ *pint milk*
⅓ *oz. yeast*	*Vanilla cream (see page* 113*)*
2 *egg yolks*	*Milk, a nut of butter*
1 *heaped tablespoon sugar*	*A little melted butter*
6 *oz. flour*	

Cream yeast with a little of the sugar, add a teaspoon of the
flour and some of the milk (tepid). Set in a warm place to
prove. Sift remaining flour into a warmed bowl, add the egg
yolks, 2 oz. melted butter, sugar, remaining milk and finally the
yeast. Beat well with a wooden spoon until smooth. Cover
with a cloth and set in a warm place to rise (about three-
quarters of an hour). Sprinkle a little flour on a pastry board,
tip the dough on to the pastry board and lightly shape into a
long roll. Cut off small rounds with a knife and set on a floured
board to rise for fifteen minutes in a warm place. Meanwhile
set the oven at Regulo 5 and light. Fill a baking dish half an

inch deep with milk. Add a small nut of butter and heat it. Put the pastry rounds in the milk, packing them not too tightly and brushing the tops with some melted butter. Cover the baking dish with a lid and bake the noodles in the oven, removing the lid towards the end of the baking time, so that the tops are nicely browned. The milk evaporates and the noodles are served hot, with vanilla cream (see page 113) poured over them.

KASTANIENREIS

Take about one pound or more chestnuts and make a slit across the top. Place chestnuts on a baking sheet and put them in a hot oven (Regulo 8) for a few minutes, until the shells come away easily. Have ready a saucepan with hot milk and a vanilla pod and drop chestnuts into milk as they are shelled (keep the chestnuts hot while shelling them—the skins are difficult to remove once the chestnuts have cooled). Simmer chestnuts in milk until soft. Drain, retaining the milk and rub chestnuts through a sieve. Cook one-eighth of a pint of the milk with three ounces of sugar until sugar spins a small thread, pour over the sieved chestnuts and beat well with a wooden spoon. Put the cooled mixture into a potato ricer and force it through the ricer straight into a glass bowl or into individual sundae glasses. Put a generous blob of sweetened whipped cream in the centre and top with a glacé cherry.

HAZEL NUT PUDDING WITH HAZEL NUT CREAM
HASELNUSSAUFLAUF MIT CREME

Butter a deep pie-dish and dust it with ground hazel nuts. Set oven at Regulo 5 and light. Toast three ounces hazel nuts on a baking sheet in the oven until skins come off easily. Rub off

the skins and grind the hazel nuts. Separate yolks and whites of
three eggs, set aside one of the yolks for the cream. Whisk the
remaining two egg yolks with one ounce sugar until thick,
whisk three egg whites until stiff, whisk in one ounce sugar.
Fold egg whites into egg yolks, together with two ounces
grated hazel nuts, one ounce flour, a little grated lemon rind,
one ounce melted butter or margarine and a pinch of cinnamon.
Bake in a pie-dish until top is nicely browned (Regulo 5) and
serve with the following sauce:

HASELNUSS CREME: (Hazel nut cream)

Put the egg yolk, half a pint of milk, one tablespoon sugar
and a vanilla pod with one teaspoon flour on top of a double
boiler. Blend until smooth and cook very carefully, stirring all
the time, until thick. Stir in the remaining one ounce hazel nuts
and remove vanilla pod.

KIPFELKOCH

The original recipe calls for the typical Austrian croissants
(*Kipfel*), but ordinary croissants will do very well indeed,
provided they are one or two days old.

5 croissants	*½ oz. breadcrumbs*
A little milk	*1 large egg*
1½ oz. butter	*1 egg yolk*
2 oz. sugar	*Lemon juice and rind*

Butter a soufflé dish or a deep pie-dish. Slice the croissants and
soak in a little milk. Cream butter and sugar, add lemon juice
and rind. Gradually add the egg and the egg yolk and the
breadcrumbs, fold in the croissants. Arrange in the buttered
dish and bake at Regulo 5 until nicely browned. Serve with
stewed fruit.

CHERRY DESSERT
KIRSCHENMEHLSPEISE

Whisk together two cups sour milk and two eggs, stir in one
cup coarse semolina and two tablespoons melted butter. Brush
a baking dish well with melted butter, pour in the semolina
mixture, sprinkle thickly with stoned cherries. Bake at
Regulo 6 until nicely browned, cut into squares and serve,
sprinkled thickly with sugar.

APRICOT DUMPLINGS
MARILLENKNOEDEL

For some reason, best known to themselves, the female
members of my family maintained that plum dumplings should
be made with a potato paste while for *Marillenknoedel* (apricot
dumplings) the special kind of paste quoted below was
obligatory. Explanations as to why this was so were not easily
forthcoming, but it appeared to be a matter of seasons: when
the plums are ripe, potatoes are usually of the right floury
consistency for making potato paste. Which does not quite
explain why the paste quoted for *Marillenknoedel* was never
used for plum dumplings!

There is, of course, no reason why the pastes should not be
switched and you might care to try the paste given on page 114
for the apricot dumplings quoted below.

Stone some apricots and replace the stone with a lump of
sugar. This is best done by easing the stone out gently—with
the help of a cooking spoon handle—without actually cutting
open the apricots. Heat three-quarters of a pint of water with
a pinch of salt and a tablespoon butter. When the water
boils, tip in half a pound of flour and stir over flame until
the dough leaves the sides of the pan clean. Remove from fire
and beat in two eggs, one after the other. Beat well with a
wooden spoon until quite smooth, put the dough into a bowl

or on a pastry board and leave to cool. When cold knead briefly just so that the dough should be smooth, then pinch off small pieces of dough and completely cover each apricot with dough, taking care that there should not be any gaps. Bring a large pan of water to the boil, add a pinch of salt and drop the dumplings into the boiling water one by one. They will sink to the bottom at once, stir carefully so that they do not stick. Cover saucepan with a lid, leaving a small gap open. Cook gently—the dumplings will rise to the top when ready. Leave to simmer for another minute or two, then lift out the dumplings very carefully, set them on a colander or a sieve and rinse under cold water. Melt three tablespoons butter in a saucepan, add four ounces good breadcrumbs and fry them until nicely browned, stirring all the time. Add the dumplings and toss them in the crumbs over low flame. Arrange dumplings and crumbs on a warmed dish, sprinkle with sugar and serve.

PANCAKES
PALATSCHINKEN

½ *pint milk*
1 *egg*
Pinch salt

About 4 oz. flour
Oil or fat for frying

Sift flour and salt into a bowl, add egg and milk gradually and whisk briskly. Some cooks add a dash of soda water at this point—it does help, but if you have no soda water you will just have to whisk the batter a little more briskly. Have ready a small jug with melted fat or a quantity of good oil. Heat a frying pan, pour in a teaspoon of melted fat or the same quantity of oil, move the pan so that the fat is spread evenly, and when it gets smoking hot pour in a little of the batter. Move pan quickly so that the mixture spreads. Shake pan a little while one side of the pancake is frying, turn pancake over and fry the other side. Use up the rest of the batter in the same way, keeping the fried pancakes warm meanwhile. You can now use a number of fillings: apricot jam is perhaps the most usual, but grated nuts and sugar, grated chocolate and nuts are equally good. Spread (or sprinkle) the filling over each pancake, roll it up and arrange the pancakes on a warmed dish. Sprinkle with sugar and serve at once. Austrian pancakes are fatter than their English counterparts, and lemon—crimped or otherwise—is not served as a matter of course.

NUSS NUDELN

Throw some noodles (the broad type, not *vermicelli*) into a large pan of boiling salt water and cook until just tender. Do not overcook, or they will be quite horrid. Drain in a colander and rinse under cold running water. Melt a tablespoon or more (depending on quantity of noodles) of butter in a saucepan and toss the noodles in this. They must not actually fry in the fat, but should be nicely covered with fat all over and thoroughly heated. Heap on a hot dish and sprinkle liberally with finely ground walnuts and sugar (mixed together). Serve at once, handing a bowl of grated walnuts and sugar separately.

Mohn Nudeln are precisely the same thing, using ground poppy seeds and sugar instead of the walnuts.

POFESEN

Trim or grate the rind off a two-day old French loaf. Cut into slices the thickness of a finger, then cut down centre of each slice to within one-eighth inch of edge and spread some nice firm jam into the opening. Dip slices into milk—or, better still, red or white wine—taking care that they should not get too wet. Dip each slice into lightly beaten egg or pancake batter (see page 103) and fry in smoking hot fat until golden brown on both sides. Drain and serve hot, dusted with sugar. Fruit syrup can be handed separately.

RICE PUDDING
REISAUFLAUF

6 oz. rice	3 oz. sugar
About ¾ pint milk	Lemon rind
Vanilla pod	Raspberries or strawberries
1 tablespoon butter	(fresh or quick-frozen,
2 eggs	drained)

Butter a soufflé dish. Wash the rice, put it in a saucepan with the butter, a vanilla pod, some lemon rind and cover with about three-quarters of a pint of milk. Cook gently until rice is soft, but not mushy. Remove from heat and leave to cool slightly. Separate egg yolks and whites. Whisk first the yolks with half the sugar until thick and creamy, then the whites until stiff. Whisk in the sugar. Fold egg whites into egg yolks. Remove vanilla pod and lemon rind from cooked rice. Fold egg mixture into rice which should by now be just tepid. Pile half the rice into the soufflé mould, arrange a layer of strawberries or raspberries over it (dust with a little sugar if using fresh fruit) and top with remaining rice. Bake at Regulo 3–4 until golden brown. Raspberry syrup should be handed separately—if using quick-frozen fruit for the pudding, serve the syrup from the fruit instead.

There are a great many versions of this recipe: apples may be used instead of strawberries or raspberries, or you can leave out the fruit altogether but stir a small handful of washed and dried raisins into the rice before baking. (Incidentally, the cooking of the rice can be done quite some time before it is finished off for baking, in fact you can use up cold left-over rice pudding in this way.) If you can spare an extra egg white, whisk it with a little sugar and top the baked pudding with this, returning it to the oven at low heat for the meringue to set.

Yet another version is to cook the rice with the vanilla pod and the lemon rind, but without the butter. The butter is creamed separately (using about half a tablespoon more than stated in the recipe) with the sugar and the egg yolks and the whipped egg whites are then folded in. The mixture is folded into the cooked rice—remaining procedure and quantities as before. This gives a slightly heavier pudding, frequently served with Vanilla cream (see page 113).

BREAD PUDDING
SCHEITERHAUFEN

8 *rolls*
½ *pint milk*
1–2 *eggs*
2 *oz. raisins*

1 *oz. chopped almonds or*
   hazel nuts
3 *oz. butter*
3 *oz. sugar*
1 *lb. apples*

Slice the rolls—which should be at least one day old. Whisk together milk and egg (or eggs) and pour over the sliced rolls. Leave to stand while peeling, coring and slicing the apples. Sprinkle apples with the sugar, raisins and chopped almonds. Arrange the sliced rolls in layers in a deep buttered pie-dish, spreading the apple mixture between each layer and dotting with butter. Finish with a layer of sliced rolls, dot with butter and bake at Regulo 5 until golden brown.

SALZBURGER NOCKERL

Quantities for two people:

3 *eggs (ideally this should*
   be 3 egg yolks and 4 egg
   whites)

1 *teaspoon icing sugar*
1 *teaspoon flour*
1 *tablespoon butter*

Set the oven at Regulo 9 and light. Put an ovenproof omelette

pan over a small flame. Separate egg yolks and whites. Whisk
the egg yolks very lightly with a fork until well blended. Whisk
egg whites until very stiff, add the icing sugar and whisk until
smooth. Fold the egg yolks into the egg whites—not the other
way round as is more usual with other recipes—then fold in
the flour. Put the butter in the omelette pan and turn up the
heat. The butter should melt at once. Wait until the butter
foams, then drop the soufflé mixture in three large 'blobs' into
the hot butter. Make the blobs high rather than wide and set
them a little apart. Leave over medium flame until underneath parts of the *Nockerln* have set—about half a minute—
then push the omelette pan quickly into the hot oven. Leave
until tops of *Nockerln* have browned lightly (this again is a
matter of minutes).

Remove *Nockerln* carefully with a palette knife and arrange
them on a hot dish. Dust liberally with icing sugar and
serve at once. The centre should be light and creamy, the outside golden brown and puffed.

SCHLOSSERBUBEN

¼ *pint beer*	*Salt*
4½ *oz. flour*	*Prunes*
1 *teaspoon oil*	*Blanched almonds*
1 *egg*	*Grated chocolate*
½ *oz. sugar*	*Deep fat for frying*

Soak the prunes in weak cold tea for one hour, remove the
stones and replace them with blanched almonds. Separate egg
yolk and white. Sift flour, salt and sugar into a bowl, blend
with the egg yolk, oil and beer. Whisk the egg white until stiff,
fold into the mixture.

Coat each prune with batter and drop into smoking hot fat,
fry until golden brown. Drain on paper and serve sprinkled
with grated chocolate.

SCHMARRN

Schmarrn means a mere nothing; a trifle tossed off easily; a favour denied.

Culinary *Schmarrn* are different. They are not trifles, but they are delicious. *Kaiserschmarrn* and *Griess Schmarrn* are perhaps the best known of all, but there is also *Semmelschmarrn* (made from rolls) and *Kipfelschmarrn*, built on a basis of croissants.

Tastes differ—you may like your *Schmarrn* soft or crisped almost to a frazzle. There is nothing like trying and tasting— and you have the wonderful consolation that nothing, absolutely nothing, can ever go wrong with a *Schmarrn*!

KAISERSCHMARRN

¼ pint milk
3 oz. flour
2 eggs

1 oz. raisins
½ tablespoon sugar
1 heaped tablespoon butter

Wash and dry the raisins. Set the oven at Regulo 6 and light. Separate egg yolks and whites. Sift flour and sugar into a bowl and stir in the milk gradually, using as much 'top of the bottle' as you can spare. Add the egg yolks and blend well; the mixture must be very smooth. Fold in the stiffly beaten egg whites. Melt the butter in a baking dish and when it begins to foam, pour in the batter and sprinkle the raisins over the top. The batter should be about one inch deep in the baking dish. Bake in the oven until nicely browned, pondering meanwhile over the question whether you want your *Kaiserschmarrn* very crisp or just a little soft. If you want it very crisp, turn it over completely with a fish slice as soon as one side is brown—it doesn't matter if it breaks in the process—and return it to the oven for a few minutes so that there is a nice crust top and bottom, then tear it into small pieces with two forks and return it to the oven for another minute or two. Serve on a hot dish, sprinkled with vanilla sugar. If you want it just a little softer, do not turn it over, but tear it into small pieces as soon as it is browned on one side, return it to the oven for a little longer and serve dusted with icing sugar as described before.

GRIESS SCHMARRN

¾ *pint milk*
5–6 *oz. coarse semolina*
2 *tablespoons butter*

Vanilla pod
½ *oz. sugar*
1 *heaped tablespoon raisins*

Put the milk, vanilla pod, sugar and a small knob of butter in a saucepan and bring to boil. Rain in the semolina, stirring constantly. Add the raisins, switch off the heat and cover the saucepan, leave it to stand for about five minutes. Meanwhile melt the remaining butter in a baking dish, pour in the semolina mixture and put it in the oven (Regulo 5). As soon as the mixture is nicely browned on top, tear it into small pieces with two forks. Return it to the oven so that the whole thing should crisp nicely, then turn it on to a warmed dish and sprinkle liberally with icing sugar. The vanilla pod can be removed either before or after the baking.

SNOWBALLS
SCHNEEBALLEN

Serve them with a little raspberry syrup as a sweet or, just sprinkled with icing sugar and a pinch of cinnamon, they will grace your tea table. The recipe for *Rosenkrapfen* (see page 146) may be used for the pastry. If you can spare an extra egg yolk, however, there is a very luxurious version:

4 oz. flour   ¼ gill white wine
2 oz. butter   A few drops rum
3 egg yolks   Deep fat for frying
½ tablespoon cream

Sift the flour on to the pastry board, make a well in the centre
and gradually add the liquid ingredients. Work to a
smooth dough with the butter, cover with a cloth and
leave for half an hour. Roll out to about one-eighth inch thickness, cut into small rectangles, using a zig-zag pastry cutter.
The rectangles should measure about four by three inches.
Run the pastry cutter three or four times down each rectangle,
from within half an inch of the edge to half an inch of the
opposite edge. Heat the fat and, when smoking hot, drop in
each snowball separately, picking up alternate strips with the
handle of a wooden cooking spoon, thus letting each 'snowball'
slide into the hot fat. Fry until golden brown, drain on
crumpled kitchen paper and dust with icing sugar while still
hot. Serve as soon as possible after frying.

SCHNEENOCKERL

Whisk four egg whites until stiff. Gradually whisk in four
tablespoons sifted icing sugar. The mixture must be very
stiff and smooth. In a large saucepan (ideally a frying pan
with a lid) heat three-quarters of a pint of milk with a
quarter of a pint of water and a vanilla pod. When the milk
begins to rise, lower heat at once and drop in the egg white
mixture with the help of a tablespoon, taking care that the
Nockerl do not touch as they swell during the cooking. Cover
with a lid and simmer gently for three minutes, the milk must
not boil. Remove lid, carefully turn the Nockerl with a palette
knife and simmer for another minute or two—this time minus
the lid. Lift out the Nockerl with a perforated spoon and
arrange them in a dish. Use up remaining egg white mixture

in the same way. Measure liquid in which the *Nockerl* were cooked and make it up to three-quarters of a pint with milk. Add three ounces sugar and heat. Slake one scant ounce flour with half a cup cold milk, whisk in three egg yolks. Gradually pour on the hot milk. Cook in a double boiler, stirring constantly, until thick. Remove vanilla pod, pour the cream over the *Nockerl* and chill well before serving.

PUDDING MADE WITH ROLLS
SEMMEL AUFLAUF

2 *rolls*	1 *tablespoon raisins*
2½ *oz. butter*	2 *eggs*
1½ *oz. sugar*	*Lemon rind and juice*
1½ *oz. ground walnuts*	*Milk*

Use rolls at least two days old. Grate off the rind and set aside one tablespoon of the fine breadcrumbs that result. Wash and dry the raisins. Soak the rolls in milk until soft, squeeze out all moisture. Cream butter and sugar, add the egg yolks gradually, then the rolls, raisins and the ground walnuts. Fold in the stiffly beaten egg whites, lemon rind and juice and finally one tablespoon breadcrumbs. Bake until golden brown (Regulo 5) in a buttered soufflé or pie-dish.

STEPHANIE OMELETTE

(Quantity sufficient for three moderate or two greedy people.)

3 *eggs*	3 *tablespoons cream*
2 *tablespoons icing sugar*	1 *dessertspoon butter*
2 *tablespoons flour*	*Apricot jam*

Light the oven at Regulo 7. Set an ovenproof omelette pan

over a very small flame to heat. Separate egg yolks and whites. Whisk egg yolks, cream and sugar until pale and creamy, whip egg whites until stiff. Fold egg whites into egg yolks, carefully add the flour. Melt butter in the omelette pan, do not let it foam—as soon as it is melted turn the pan round and round so that bottom and sides are well covered with the melted butter. Put the omelette mixture into the pan, spreading it so that it is slightly higher round the sides—this makes the folding over easier. Put the omelette into the hot oven as quickly as possible and leave to brown. This takes about eight minutes, by which time the omelette should be nicely puffed up and golden brown. Spread quickly with warmed apricot jam and slide on to a sugared, warmed dish, folding the omelette over at the same time. Dust top with sugar and serve at once. Thawed quick-frozen strawberries or raspberries, drained, also make an excellent filling.

CREAM CHEESE TURN-OVERS
TOPFENTASCHERL

Prepare a stiff paste with seven ounces flour, one egg, salt and about one-eighth pint water. Roll out thinly and stamp into rounds. Cream two and a half ounces butter with one heaped tablespoon sugar, add one egg, four to six ounces cream cheese, and sufficient milk or sour milk to give a stiff paste. Stir in a few washed and dried raisins. Put a good dab of filling in centre of each pastry round, brush round the filling with egg and fold over pastry, pressing down the edges. Cook in boiling salt water for about eight minutes, drain and rinse under cold tap. Toss in hot butter and sprinkle thickly with sugar and cinnamon before serving.

VANILLA CREAM
VANILLE CREME

To be served with hot or cold puddings.

¾ pint milk	2 egg yolks or 1 whole egg
Vanilla pod	3 oz. sugar
1 tablespoon cornflour	

Whisk together sugar, egg yolks, cornflour and a little of the cold milk. Heat remaining milk with the vanilla pod and pour over other ingredients, stirring all the time. Return mixture to stove on top of a double boiler and cook until thick, stirring all the time.

WINE PUDDING
WEINKOCH

A good substantial sweet for a cold day—quantities may be halved if necessary.

4 eggs	2 oz. sugar
2 oz. ground unblanched almonds	1 oz. biscuit crumbs
	Grated lemon rind

also:

¼ pint white wine	1 clove
Vanilla pod	Juice and rind of ½ lemon
2½ oz. sugar	¼ pint water

Butter a deep pie-dish and sprinkle it with ground almonds. Separate egg yolks and whites. Whisk egg yolks with one ounce of sugar until thick and creamy. Whisk egg whites until stiff, fold in the remaining one ounce sugar and whisk again. Fold egg whites into egg yolks, fold in the ground almonds and the crumbs, sprinkle in the grated lemon rind. Bake at Regulo 6 until nicely browned (about twenty to twenty-five minutes). While the pudding is baking, put two and a half ounces of sugar in a saucepan and melt over a low flame. When the sugar turns pale yellow, add the wine, water, vanilla pod, clove, lemon juice and rind. Heat well and strain hot over the baked pudding. Serve at once.

WIENER KOCH

⅜ pint milk   2 oz. vanilla sugar
3 eggs   1 tablespoon flour
1½ oz. butter

Light oven at Regulo 7 and prepare a soufflé dish as described on page 115. Separate egg yolks and whites. Blend together flour and egg yolks, add a little cold milk. Heat remaining milk with the butter and stir into egg yolks, etc. Return mixture to stove in a double boiler and cook very gently, stirring constantly until thick. Remove from fire, stir until cool. Fold in stiffly beaten egg whites and bake for about twelve minutes.

PLUM DUMPLINGS
ZWETSCHKENKNOEDEL

Use the small blue plums which look rather like outsize damsons. Some Soho greengrocers even sell them under the name *Zwetschken*. Stone the plums and replace the stone with a lump of sugar.

Boil one pound of potatoes in their skins, using floury potatoes. Skin while still hot and push them through a sieve straight on to the pastry board. Leave to cool, then add a pinch of salt, one egg (or two egg yolks), two tablespoons butter and sufficient flour to make a dough which does not stick to the pastry board. The quantity of the flour varies according to the quality of potatoes, it may be anything between five and eight ounces and it is therefore absolutely necessary to make a test with one dumpling before covering all the plums with dough. Cover the dough with a cloth and leave for half an hour. Pinch a small piece off the dough and wrap it round a plum, being careful that there are no gaps. Drop it into a large pan of boiling salted water, see that it does not stick to the bottom of the pan and cover the pan with a lid, leaving a small gap open. The dumpling will rise to the top when cooked. Fish it out with a perforated spoon and cut it open. If the dough was too soft, add a little more flour (or fine semolina). If it was too stiff, work in a little more egg. Cover each plum with a little of the dough, carefully sealing all openings. Roll each dumpling between the palms of your hands to ensure it is quite smooth. Drop dumplings into boiling salted water, stir so that they do not stick to the bottom of the pan and cook gently until dumplings rise to the top (this takes about ten to twelve minutes according to size). Cook in a covered saucepan, with the lid slightly tilted. Simmer for another minute after dumplings have risen to the top, then drain on a colander or a sieve, rinse under cold water. Melt three good tablespoons butter in a saucepan, stir in four ounces breadcrumbs and brown. Add the dumplings and toss them in the breadcrumbs over a small flame. Arrange dumplings on a hot dish, sprinkle with sugar and serve.

BAKED SOUFFLÉS

TO PREPARE A SOUFFLÉ DISH:

Butter the dish well, then tie a piece of buttered paper round it to come about two inches over the top. Dust the soufflé dish —including the paper—with icing sugar. For the Strawberry

Soufflé I like to substitute ground almonds or hazel nuts for
the sugar. The paper is of course removed just before serving
and—need I say it—soufflés are best consumed within a one-
yard radius of the oven in which they were cooked!

CAUTIONARY WARNING:

With Soufflés, almost more than with any other kind of dish,
the idiosyncrasies of one's oven are important and simply have
to be studied. Times and temperatures given apply to my own
oven and you may find that they have to be varied slightly
when applied elsewhere.

'LADIES' SOUFFLÉ'
DAMEN AUFLAUF

Prepare a Soufflé dish as described above and light the
oven at Regulo 7. Break one ounce vanilla chocolate into small
pieces and put in a warm place to melt. Separate yolks and
whites of three eggs. Whisk the egg yolks with two and a half
ounces icing sugar, add the melted chocolate and finally fold
in the stiffly beaten whites of the three eggs. Bake for about
twelve minutes and serve at once—with hot chocolate sauce,
if you are really greedy.

STRAWBERRY SOUFFLÉ
ERDBEER AUFLAUF

Heat oven at Regulo 7 and prepare soufflé mould as described
above. Put three ounces unsweetened strawberry purée
(made from about five ounces fresh strawberries crushed
through a sieve), two and a half ounces granulated sugar and
one egg white in a bowl. Stir, like creaming butter and sugar
for a cake, until the mixture is thick and almost stiff. Whisk
three egg whites until stiff, fold in one tablespoon granulated

sugar, whisk for another minute until smooth. Fold whipped egg whites into strawberry mixture and pile into the soufflé mould. Sprinkle with a few ground almonds or hazel nuts and bake at Regulo 7 for ten minutes, turn down heat to 5½ without opening oven door. Bake for another seven minutes, serve at once.

SOUFFLÉ ROTHSCHILD

Quantity for two persons:

¼ *pint milk*	2 *egg yolks*
Vanilla pod	3 *egg whites*
1 *tablespoon butter*	3 *oz. glacé fruits*
2 *tablespoons sugar*	*A little Kirsch*
1½ *oz. flour*	

Light oven at Regulo 7 and prepare a soufflé dish as described on page 115. Put milk, one tablespoon sugar and one tablespoon butter in a saucepan, add a vanilla pod and bring to boil. Cut the glacé fruit into equal-sized chunks and moisten with a little Kirsch. When the milk boils, take out the vanilla pod and quickly stir in the flour, stirring the mixture over a low flame until it leaves the sides of the saucepan clean. Remove from fire, gradually beat in the egg yolks and when cool, fold in the egg whites whipped up stiff with the sugar, and finally the glacé fruit. Pile into the soufflé dish and bake for about ten to twelve minutes. Serve with vanilla cream (see page 113).

LEMON SOUFFLÉ
ZITRONEN AUFLAUF

Light the oven at Regulo 6 and prepare a soufflé mould as described on page 115, dusting it very well with icing sugar.

Separate yolks and whites of five eggs. Whisk the yolks with three ounces icing sugar and the juice and grated rind of one lemon. When thick and creamy, fold in the stiffly beaten whites of five eggs. Pile into the soufflé dish and bake for about twelve minutes. Dust with icing sugar, remove paper and serve at once.

STEAMED PUDDINGS

Whether you prefer to make one large pudding or divide the mixture into several small moulds is a matter of taste—and convenience. The mould (or moulds) must be well buttered, then sprinkled with sugar or ground hazel nuts, almonds or fine crumbs. This is infinitely preferable to flouring the mould. Never fill the moulds more than three-quarters full. Special moulds for steamed puddings are now sold which have a well-fitting lid. This is not really necessary, as long as the lid of the steamer fits well, but I always put a round of buttered paper on top of the pudding mixture to stop any condensed steam dripping into the pudding.

YELLOW PUDDING WITH CHOCOLATE SAUCE
GELBER PUDDING MIT SCHOKOLADE SAUCE

3½ oz. butter   Rind and juice of ¼ lemon
3 eggs   3 tablespoons flour
4 oz. sugar

Separate egg yolks and whites. Cream butter (or margarine) and sugar, add yolks gradually. Fold in flour alternately with stiffly beaten egg whites. Add lemon rind and juice. Steam for about three-quarters to one hour. Serve with the following sauce.

SCHOKOLADE SAUCE: (Chocolate Sauce)

Break four ounces plain chocolate into small pieces. Dissolve chocolate in a half pint of water together with four ounces of sugar and cook until thickened. Serve separately.

HAZEL NUT PUDDING
HASELNUSS PUDDING

3 eggs
2 oz. butter
2 oz. sugar

2 oz. hazel nuts
1 oz. biscuit crumbs
1 oz. flour, grated lemon rind

Separate egg yolks and whites. Cream butter with half the sugar and the egg yolks. Add egg yolks. Whisk egg whites until stiff, whisk in remaining sugar. Fold egg whites into butter, add ground hazel nuts, crumbs and flour. Stir in grated lemon rind. Steam as described on page 118. Prepare the following sauce:

HAZEL NUT AND RUM SAUCE:

½ pint milk
2 egg yolks
2 oz. sugar

2 oz. toasted hazel nuts
1 tablespoon rum

Place all ingredients except the hazel nuts in a bowl and whisk over steam until thick. Remove from fire and stir in ground hazel nuts. Hand sauce separately.

COFFEE PUDDING
KAFFEEPUDDING

3 oz. rolls (weight after
    cutting off rinds)
¼ pint strong black coffee
3 oz. butter

3 eggs
3 oz. icing sugar
2½ oz. ground almonds
    (not blanched)

Pour hot black coffee over rolls, stir well, then pass through a
sieve. Separate egg yolks and whites. Cream butter with sugar,
add egg yolks and rolls. Fold in stiffly beaten egg whites
alternately with the ground almonds. Steam for about three-
quarters of an hour. Serve with wine sauce as for almond
pudding.

ALMOND PUDDING
MANDEL PUDDING

4 *eggs*
2¼ *oz. sugar*
2 *oz. flour*

2½ *oz. ground almonds*
1 *oz. melted butter*

Separate egg yolks and whites. Whisk yolks with half the sugar
until fluffy. Whisk egg whites until stiff. Fold sugar into egg
whites, then fold whites into yolks, alternately with flour and
ground almonds. Fold in melted butter. Steam for about
20–25 minutes. Serve with the following sauce:

WHITE WINE SAUCE:

¼ *pint white wine*
2 *eggs*

Juice of ½ *lemon*
2½ *oz. sugar*

Put all ingredients in a bowl and whisk over steam until light
and bubbly. Serve separately.

MOHR IM HEMD

4 *eggs*
2¼ *oz. butter*
2¼ *oz. sugar*

2¼ *oz. chocolate*
2¼ *oz. ground almonds*

Butter pudding mould and dust with icing sugar. Separate egg
yolks and whites. Cream butter with sugar until light and
fluffy. Beat in egg yolks one after the other. Whip egg whites

until stiff. Fold whipped egg whites into creamed butter, alternately with the ground almonds and chocolate. Fill into prepared mould. Steam for about forty minutes. Should be served with sweetened whipped cream—on special occasions with chocolate sauce (see Yellow Pudding, page 118) *and* whipped cream. Can be eaten hot or cold.

NUT PUDDING
NUSSPUDDING

4 eggs
5 oz. ground walnuts
1 heaped tablespoon fine
   breadcrumbs
2½ oz. sugar

3 oz. butter
2 small brioches
A tiny pinch Nescafé
A little milk

If the brioches (day-old for preference) are not available, a small roll, minus the crust, will do. Prepare a pudding basin as described on page 118. Separate egg yolks and whites. Soak the brioches (or roll) in milk until soft, squeeze out the moisture and crumble the roll between the fingers. Cream butter and sugar, add the egg yolks and the crumbled brioches. Fold in stiffly whipped egg whites, ground walnuts, breadcrumbs and a tiny pinch Nescafé. Steam in pudding mould as described on page 118. Serve with whipped cream or fruit syrup.

RUM PUDDING
RUM PUDDING

2½ oz. butter
2½ oz. sugar
3 eggs
2½ oz. ground almonds (*not*
   blanched)

2½ oz. raisins
1 oz. chocolate
1 scant oz. breadcrumbs
   moistened with rum

Separate egg yolks and whites. Cream butter and sugar, add egg yolks gradually. Fold in stiffly whipped egg whites alternately with ground almonds, chocolate and crumbs. Stir in raisins. Steam for about three quarters of an hour.

RUM SAUCE:

Whisk over steam three tablespoons rum, two egg yolks and a little sugar until frothy. Pour over pudding or hand separately.

CHOCOLATE PUDDING
SCHOKOLADE PUDDING

2 oz. butter	3 eggs
1½ oz. sugar	1½ rolls
1½ oz. toasted ground almonds	1 oz. chocolate

Cut rinds off rolls, cut rolls into cubes and soak in milk. Separate egg yolks and whites. Cream butter and sugar, add egg yolks gradually. Drain rolls, squeeze out moisture and add. Whisk egg whites until stiff, fold into mixture, also fold in grated chocolate and ground almonds. Steam for about three-quarters of an hour.

To lift this pudding right into the luxury class, serve with the following:

CHOCOLATE SAUCE WITH WHIPPED CREAM:

Break four ounces chocolate into small pieces and melt in oven. Melt four tablespoons sugar in two tablespoons water and cook to 'small thread' stage. Remove from fire and stir into melted chocolate. Stir until cool, but still spreadable, then fold in a quarter of a pint of whipped cream.

CAKES, PASTRIES AND BISCUITS

*

THE culinary repertoire of Austria boasts many cake and biscuit recipes. Some are rich and rare and require an army of helpers to reach perfection. Others are so simple that it seems presumptuous even to write down the recipe. Most of them are widely known and where this is the case, there are also many variations regarding the preparation of one and the same thing. Thus there are numerous recipes concerning *Guglhupf*, or *Bischofsbrot*, or the hundred and one different yet similar nut and almond biscuits.

I have tried to be discriminating and yet fair to recipes which I have known and loved since I can remember. If I have seemingly repeated myself—it was done in the firm belief that a box overflowing with home-made biscuits is better than all the shop-bought cakes in the world!

APPLE FLAN
APFEL PASTETE

Sift together two ounces of sugar and five ounces of flour. Crumble five ounces of butter or margarine into sugar and flour, add two and a half ounces ground almonds (unblanched), a few drops lemon juice and one whole egg. Pat into a round and chill for half an hour. Line bottom and sides of a buttered and floured sandwich tin with this pastry, bake 'blind' (Regulo 5). Meanwhile peel and slice three apples and put the slices in a saucepan. Dust with sugar, add a few raisins, about one tablespoon ground and blanched almonds and a dash of rum. Simmer very gently—no water—for about five minutes. Remove from stove and leave to cool. Whisk one large egg white until stiff, add one ounce caster sugar, whisk again until smooth. Fold in another one and a half ounces of caster sugar. Fill pastry shell with the apples and with a forcing bag pipe

a criss-cross pattern of the meringue mixture over the top.
Put in a cool oven (Regulo 1) until meringue has set.

APPLE SLICES
APFELSCHNITTEN

Prepare a short crust with nine ounces flour, six ounces butter
or margarine, three tablespoons sugar, three tablespoons 'top
milk', one egg yolk and a little grated lemon rind. Divide pastry
into two equal parts and chill for fifteen minutes. After that
time, knead pastry a little so that it is perfectly smooth, roll out
on a floured pastry board into two equal-sized pieces. Put one
sheet of pastry on a buttered and floured baking sheet, cover
thickly with sliced apples, sprinkle with sugar and raisins and
place other sheet of pastry on top. Prick lightly with a fork
brush with egg white and bake until golden brown (Regulo 4½).
Cut into slices when cold and dust with icing sugar.

APPLE STRUDEL
APFELSTRUDEL

Strudel pastry as described on　　　1 *cup sugar*
   page 151　　　　　　　　　　1½ *cups breadcrumbs*
FILLING:　　　　　　　　　　　*Butter for frying*
1 *lb. cooking apples*　　　　　　　*Apricot jam*
¾ *cup raisins*　　　　　　　　　　*A little melted butter*

Prepare *Strudel* pastry as described on page 151. Peel, core
and thinly slice the apples. Clean the raisins and add to the
apples, sprinkle with sugar. Set aside in a bowl and cover it.
Fry breadcrumbs in butter. Sprinkle the fried breadcrumbs
evenly over the pastry, then spread the apple and raisin filling
over half the surface only, sprinkle with melted butter and dot
with a little apricot jam. Tear off the rather thick rim which

overhangs the table and start rolling the *Strudel* by lifting the cloth at the 'apple' end. Roll up very carefully, like a Swiss roll, close up ends and place on a buttered baking sheet, forming a horseshoe. Brush with melted butter and cover with greaseproof paper. Bake in a moderate oven (Regulo 4–4½) for about three-quarters of an hour, removing paper towards the end. Sprinkle with vanilla sugar while still warm.

BISHOP'S BREAD I
BISCHOFSBROT I

3 *eggs and their weight in*
  sugar and flour
2 *oz. dried figs*
2 *oz. walnuts*
2 *oz. dates*

2 *oz. unblanched almonds*
2 *oz. hazel nuts*
2 *oz. candied peel*
A little lemon juice and
  grated lemon rind

Chop fruit and nuts. Separate egg yolks and whites. Whisk egg yolks with sugar, fold in the stiffly beaten egg whites alternately with the flour. Finally fold in lemon juice, lemon rind and fruit and nuts. Bake in an oblong buttered and floured cake tin (Regulo 4½). Cool on a rack and cut into thin slices when cold.

BISHOP'S BREAD II
BISCHOFSBROT II

2 *eggs*
3½ *oz. butter*
3½ *oz. flour*
3½ *oz. sugar*

A little grated lemon rind
2 *oz. washed and dried raisins*
2 *oz. chocolate*
2 *oz. almonds or walnuts*
2 *oz. glacé cherries*

Separate egg yolks and whites. Chop chocolate and almonds. (Chocolate can also be broken into small lumps.) Cream butter with half the sugar, add the egg yolks and cream well. Whisk egg whites until stiff, whisk in remaining sugar. Fold beaten egg whites into egg yolks alternately with the flour. Add lemon rind, raisins, almonds, glacé cherries and chocolate gradually and bake in a buttered and floured oblong tin (Regulo 4) for about forty-five minutes. Cool on a rack and slice when cold.

'BEE'S STING'
BIENENSTICH

9 oz. flour
3½ oz. butter or margarine
1½ oz. sugar
3 tablespoons milk
Pinch baking powder

3½ oz. butter
3½ oz. vanilla sugar
2 oz. ground almonds

Sift together flour, sugar and baking powder. Work to a dough with the butter (or margarine) and the milk. Pat into a round and cover with a cloth.

Melt the butter over a low flame until it begins to get 'oily'. Stir in the ground almonds and the vanilla sugar and continue stirring over low flame until the mixture is smooth and creamy. Remove from fire, stir until cool. Roll out the dough to a quarter-inch thickness. Line a buttered and floured baking sheet with the pastry, spread the almond mixture over it and bake at Regulo 4 for about thirty-five minutes.

Note: A foundation of yeast pastry is sometimes used in place of the pastry quoted above—cut once and filled with vanilla cream and topped as described before.

PUFF PASTRY
BLAETTERTEIG

No two women will ever quite agree about the way to make

puff pastry. The method quoted below (cribbed by my grandmother from a retired *patissier* who came to live in our village)
has two virtues: it is comparatively quick (as puff pastry goes
—and not counting the 'resting' times) and safe. And what
more can one want?

9 oz. flour	1 *tablespoon lemon juice or*
9 oz. butter	*wine vinegar*
About ¼ pint water	*Pinch salt*

(Our friend the *patissier* used dry white wine instead of lemon
juice and water.)

Sift together flour and salt. Crumble the butter into three
ounces flour, knead until smooth. Shape into a brick, trim off
edges with a knife and keep the trimmings on one side. Cover
the butter brick with a cloth wrung out in cold water, set it
aside in a cool place, but do not put in a refrigerator. Sift the remaining six ounces flour on to a pastry board, make a well in
the centre and pour in a little of the water and the lemon juice.
Draw the flour towards the middle, gradually adding the
remaining water. Add the trimmings from the butter brick and
knead really well until dough is very smooth and pliable. Pat
into a round, make a cross-like incision on top with a knife,
cover with a cloth wrung out in cold water and leave for half
an hour. After that time roll it out on a very lightly floured
pastry board to a strip three times as long and about two inches
wider than the butter brick. The pastry should be slightly
thicker in the middle, tapering off towards the sides. Place
butter brick in centre, fold edges over so that the brick is completely covered with pastry and beat with a rolling pin from
the centre outwards, then roll into a strip. (Some cooks prefer
to roll out the dough first into a square, placing the butter
brick in the centre and folding over the outer dough, pinching
together the edges well—rather like completely opening up and
closing an envelope. Both ways work equally well). Fold the
pastry strip into three, cover with a cloth wrung out in cold

water and leave in a cool place for fifteen minutes. Roll out dough into a strip, fold both sides towards the middle, then fold together—rather like closing a book. Cover with a cloth and leave in a cool place for half an hour. Roll out into a strip, fold into three parts as before, leave under a damp cloth for ten minutes, then roll it out and fold sides towards middle, fold over as before. Leave in a cool place (under a damp cloth) for at least half an hour before use.

Bake at Regulo 6½ (unless otherwise stated in the recipe), oven pre-heated for fifteen to twenty minutes.

The following points are important:

(1) Do not butter and flour the baking sheet—rinse it in cold water and do not wipe it dry.

(2) When cutting the pastry into required shapes, use a hot, wet cutter or knife. The best way to handle this is to stand knife or cutter in a jug of hot water by the side of the pastry board.

(3) When the pastry is 'resting' it must always be covered with a cloth previously wrung out in cold water.

(4) When rolling and folding the pastry, use as little flour on the pastry board as possible and always brush it off the pastry (I do not actually brush, but blow it off—unprofessional, but it works!).

(5) Where the recipe says 'brush top of pastry with egg or milk' be careful that only the top of the pastry is thus treated. Under no circumstances must the liquid run down the sides, as this prevents rising.

(6) Cool away from all draughts—a warm kitchen or in the oven with the heat switched off and the door opened, are the best places.

CREAM SLICES
CREMESCHNITTEN

Prepare puff pastry as described on page 126. Roll out to about quarter-inch thickness, cut into strips about four inches wide and bake as described on page 128. When cold cut into one and a half inch wide slices and sandwich two together with either of the following creams; dust top with icing sugar or cover with thin white water icing.

CREAM FILLING I:

½ pint milk

2 egg yolks

Vanilla pod

⅓ oz. gelatine

1 tablespoon potato flour

2 oz. sugar

Dissolve the gelatine in a little hot water and leave to cool. Blend egg yolks with the potato flour, the sugar and a little cold milk. Heat the remaining milk with vanilla pod and add it gradually to the egg yolks, etc. Whisk over steam until thick, remove from fire and add the dissolved gelatine. Whisk until cool, remove the vanilla pod and chill cream before using.

CREAM FILLING II:

3 egg yolks

2½ oz. sugar

Vanilla pod

¼ pint cream

½ teaspoon cornflour

Mix together egg yolks, sugar and cornflour, add the vanilla pod and whisk over steam until thick. Remove from fire and whisk until cool. Whip the cream and fold it into the egg mixture, remove the vanilla pod.

'ENGLISH BREAD'
ENGLISCHES BROT

½ lb. flour

¼ lb. sugar

¼ lb. butter

1 hard-boiled egg yolk

1 egg yolk

Jam

About 1 tablespoon sugar

½ cup currants

½ cup blanched almonds

Sift together flour and sugar. Cut butter into small pieces, crumble into dry ingredients (flour, sugar and hard-boiled egg yolk). Knead to a dough, roll out as thinly as possible (about one-eighth inch) and bake at Regulo 4½ until golden brown. Spread with jam while still warm and cut into two equal parts. Leave to cool on a rack. Place one sheet of pastry on top of the other so that the jam is in the centre. Cream egg yolk with about one tablespoon sugar, spread over top of pastry. Sprinkle with blanched almonds cut into strips and with currants and dry in warm oven (Regulo 2).

GUGLHUPF MIT BACKPULVER

Guglhupf can be made with yeast (see page 164, also for general remarks about *Guglhupf* forms) and with baking powder. If made with the latter, there are various delectable varieties—it may be a *Gewoehnlicher Backpulver Guglhupf* (an ordinary *Guglhupf* made with baking powder), a *Rahmguglhupf* (*Guglhupf* made with cream or at least 'top milk'), or a *Marmor Guglhupf* (marbled *Guglhupf* where the mixture is divided into two parts and a little grated or melted chocolate is added to one half. *Marmor Guglhupf* can also be made of a yeast mixture). In special cases—and for special occasions—it may even be a *Sacher Guglhupf*, a particularly good mixture made without raisins and almonds, but covered with chocolate icing after baking.

3½ oz. butter	4 tablespoons milk
5 oz. sugar	Grated rind of ½ lemon
5 eggs	Blanched almonds
10 oz. flour	½ cup washed and dried
2 teaspoons baking powder	raisins

Prepare *Guglhupf* mould as described on page 163. Cream butter and sugar. Sift together flour and baking powder. Add

well beaten eggs to butter, alternately with flour and milk.
Fold in grated lemon rind and the raisins. Bake at Regulo 4½
for about one hour. Dust with icing sugar while still warm.

BRANDY RINGS
COGNAC RINGERL

1 egg yolk
2½ oz. sugar
5 oz. flour
5 oz. butter
5 oz. ground almonds or
    walnuts

Rind of 1 lemon
2 tablespoons brandy
Pinch cinnamon
Icing sugar, brandy

Sift together sugar and flour, add the ground almonds.
Crumble butter into dry ingredients, add the egg yolk, brandy,
cinnamon and lemon rind and knead to a smooth dough. Chill
for a quarter of an hour. Roll out to about a quarter-inch
thickness, cut into rings and set them on a buttered and
floured baking sheet. Brush the rings with brandy and dust
with icing sugar, add a few more drops of brandy so that they
are covered with a thick layer of sugar moistened with brandy.
Bake at Regulo 4 until golden brown.

BUTTER RINGS
BUTTER RINGERL

3½ oz. flour
2½ oz. butter
½ cup cream
½ tablespoon rum

Chopped blanched almonds
A little granulated sugar
Egg for brushing over pastry

Sift flour on to a pastry board. Cut butter into small lumps.
Make a well in the centre of the flour, pour in cream and

the rum. Add the butter and work to a smooth dough with a palette knife. Pat into a round and chill for fifteen minutes. Roll out to about a quarter-inch thickness and cut into rings, using two circular biscuit cutters of different sizes. Set pastry rings on a buttered and floured baking sheet, bake at Regulo 5 until pale golden brown (about fifteen minutes). Take out of oven, brush with egg, sprinkle with sugar and chopped almonds and return to oven. Switch off the heat and leave biscuits to dry in the oven.

HAZEL NUT BISCUITS
HASELNUSS BAECKEREI

2 egg whites
3 oz. caster sugar

2 oz. toasted hazel nuts
(weighed after skins
have been rubbed off)

Place about two and a half ounces of hazel nuts on a baking sheet and put in hot oven (Regulo 7). Test after a few minutes —the skins should rub off easily. Put hazel nuts in a clean cloth, rub off the skins. Grind hazel nuts.

Whisk egg whites until stiff, whisk in half the sugar, fold in remaining sugar alternately with the ground hazel nuts. With the aid of a forcing bag pipe small shapes on to a buttered and floured baking sheet. Bake at Regulo 2 until lightly tinged with colour.

HAZEL NUT STICKS
HASELNUSS STENGERL

3½ oz. butter
4½ oz. sugar
2 egg yolks

5½ oz. flour
Ground or finely chopped
hazel nuts

Cream butter and sugar, work in egg yolk and flour. Knead dough on a pastry board, roll out to one-eighth-inch thickness.

Cut pastry into strips, brush with remaining egg yolk and sprinkle with hazel nuts. Bake on buttered and floured baking sheet until golden brown (Regulo 5).

FLORENTINER

2 egg whites
2½ oz. icing sugar
3 oz. grated chocolate
5 oz. blanched almonds cut
    into strips

ICING:
1 teaspoon butter
2 oz. chocolate

Whisk egg whites until stiff. Whisk in half the sugar, fold in remaining sugar carefully, together with the grated chocolate and the blanched almonds. Place small heaps of this mixture on a buttered baking sheet, well apart. Bake at Regulo 2 until light brown in colour and dry. Remove from oven, let cool a little, then remove from baking sheet and place upside down on a rack. Melt chocolate, stir in the butter and mix well. When the biscuits are cool, spread with chocolate, mark with a fork. Leave to dry, then arrange on a plate with the chocolate side down.

FILLED HONEYCAKES
GEFUELLTE LEBKUCHEN

¼ lb. honey
2 oz. sugar
1 dessertspoon cinnamon
Pinch ground cloves
½ lb. flour
1 egg
½ teaspoon baking powder
Halved blanched almonds

Egg white for brushing over
    pastry

FILLING:
2 oz. ground hazel nuts
2 oz. sugar
1 oz. mixed peel (chopped)
1 egg

Heat honey, then add cinnamon, cloves and sugar. Stir well and leave to cool. Add flour, previously sifted with the baking powder, and the egg. Knead well, cover with a cloth and leave overnight. Mix together all ingredients for the filling. Roll out dough to about one-eighth inch thickness, cut into shapes and spread half of them with the filling. Place remaining honey-cakes over the ones spread with filling, brush with egg white and decorate with halved blanched almonds. Bake at Regulo 3½.

GERSTNERKRAPFEN

2 *eggs*	*Glacé fruit*
2 *oz. sugar*	*Rum*
2 *oz. flour*	*Raspberry or strawberry jam*
½ *oz. melted butter*	*Thin white water icing*

Set oven at Regulo 8 and light. Place eggs and sugar in a bowl and whisk over steam until thick and fluffy. Remove from fire, whisk until cool, fold in flour and lemon rind, finally fold in melted butter. Turn heat down to Regulo 6. Spread mixture to thickness of a finger on a buttered and floured baking sheet and bake until golden brown (about ten to fifteen minutes). Cut into rounds with a pastry cutter while still hot (dip pastry cutter into flour from time to time), remove pastry from baking sheet and set to cool on a sieve. For each round of pastry allow one-third of an ounce of glacé fruit, moistened with rum and bound with a little jam. Arrange glacé fruit in centre of each round, cover with thin white water icing and leave to dry.

GLEICHHEITSKUCHEN

3 *eggs, their weight in sugar*	*Cherries, redcurrants or*
Flour and butter	*grapes*

Wash and dry the fruit on a sieve. Dust the fruit very lightly

with flour. Separate egg yolks and whites. Cream butter and
sugar, add egg yolks gradually. Fold in the stiffly beaten egg
whites alternately with the flour. The mixture is very stiff
indeed.

Spread cake mixture in a buttered and floured cake tin
(tradition has it that it should be an oblong one) and place
the floured fruit on top, pressing it down very lightly. Bake
at Regulo 5 (this usually takes just over an hour). Ease
the cake a little from the sides of the cake tin and leave in
the oven with the heat switched off and the door slightly
open for about fifteen minutes, then turn the cake carefully on
to a sieve and leave it to cool, fruit side uppermost. It is served
dusted thickly with vanilla sugar.

HUSARENKRAPFERL

2½ oz. sugar   *A little grated lemon rind*
5 oz. butter   *Jam*
6½ oz. flour   *Egg for brushing over pastry*
1 egg yolk

Sift together sugar and flour, add grated lemon rind. Crumble
butter into dry ingredients, add the egg yolk and knead to a
smooth dough. Pat into a round and chill for about twenty
to thirty minutes. Pinch small lumps off the dough and roll
into balls between the palms of the hands. Set these balls
on a buttered and floured baking sheet. With the handle of a
wooden cooking spoon (dipped into flour from time to time)
make a dent in the centre of each pastry ball—this will spread
it a little. Brush pastry with egg—a few chopped blanched
almonds sprinkled over the pastry before baking greatly
enhance the taste—and bake at Regulo 4½-5 until golden
brown. Remove from baking sheet while still warm and put
a small dab of jam in the centre of each round. Dust with
vanilla sugar.

ISCHLER KRAPFEN

4 oz. butter	Raspberry or redcurrant jam,
4 oz. flour	chocolate icing
2 oz. sugar	A few hazel nuts
2 oz. ground hazel nuts, walnuts or almonds (not blanched)	

Mix together all dry ingredients, crumble butter into these and work to a smooth dough. Pat into a round and chill for at least half an hour, longer if possible. Roll out to one-eighth-inch thickness, stamp into rounds and bake on buttered and floured baking sheet (Regulo 5). Remove from baking sheet and cool on a rack. When cold sandwich two and two together with jam and cover top (not sides) with chocolate icing or melted chocolate. Place a hazel nut in centre of each round. At the famous Zauner *patisserie* in Ischl, where these Krapfen originated, and are still served as a *specialité de la maison*, they are always sandwiched together with very good chocolate butter icing.

CHESTNUT SLICES
KASTANIENSCHNITTEN

Prepare and bake mixture as for *Zigeunerschnitten* (see page 156). Cut into two-inch wide strips and sprinkle with sherry or brandy. Whip one-eighth pint cream until stiff and fold into six ounces sweetened chestnut purée, add a few drops of Maraschino and spread thickly over the cake base. Sprinkle with some biscuit crumbs and chill while preparing chocolate icing (see page 199). Spread icing carefully over the chestnut cream, chill again, then cut into slices.

Sweetened Chestnut purée can be bought in good stores and Soho shops. If not available, use cooked and sieved chestnuts beaten to a cream with a little 'top milk' and icing sugar to taste.

'HEDGEHOGS'
IGEL

For this you need about seven or eight small sponge cake rounds—about two inches in diameter and half an inch high. Set sponge cakes on a flat dish, sprinkle with a little liqueur or brandy and chill lightly. Cream two ounces butter with one tablespoon sugar. Gradually add one egg yolk, beat mixture well, then add very gradually—almost drop by drop—two tablespoons strong black coffee. Pile a little of the cream on top of each sponge round, spike with toasted blanched almonds cut into strips.

CHILDREN'S TEACAKE
KINDERZWIEBACK

2 *eggs*	2 *tablespoons flour*
2 *tablespoons sugar*	¼ *teaspoon baking powder*

Sift together flour and baking powder, sift again. Separate egg yolks and whites. Whisk egg yolks with sugar until thick and creamy. Whip egg whites until stiff. Fold egg whites into egg yolks, alternately with the flour. Bake in a buttered and floured oblong cake tin (Regulo 3). Remove from tin while still hot and cool on a rack. Next day cut into ¼-inch slices and toast in oven on both sides. Serve sprinkled with vanilla.

CRESCENTS
KIPFERL AUS ZUCKERTEIG

2 *oz. butter*	1 *teaspoon lemon juice*
4 *oz. flour*	1½ *oz. sugar*
1 *egg yolk*	

Sift together flour and sugar, crumble butter into the dry

ingredients and knead to a smooth dough with the egg yolk and lemon juice. Roll small pieces of the dough between the palms of the hands, shape into crescents or letters of the alphabet. Bake on a buttered and floured sheet (Regulo 4½) until golden brown. Dust with icing sugar while still hot.

LINZERSCHNITTEN

PASTRY:
9 oz. flour
7 oz. butter
9 oz. sugar
1 egg yolk
A little lemon juice and rind

FILLING:
¼ pint cream
1½ oz. sugar
2 oz. grated chocolate

Sift together flour and sugar, crumble butter into this. Knead to a smooth dough with the egg yolk and lemon juice and rind. Roll out to quarter-inch thickness, bake on buttered and floured baking sheet at Regulo 5. Cut into slices while still warm. Whip cream until stiff, whisk in the sugar. Set aside a little of the whipped cream for decoration. Fold grated chocolate into remaining cream and spread half the pastry slices with this. Top with remaining slices and decorate with small blobs of whipped cream. Dust icing sugar over the top.

ALMOND 'BREAD'
MANDELBROT

10 oz. flour
4½ oz. butter
3½ oz. chopped blanched
   almonds

3 oz. sugar
1 egg yolk
A little milk

Crumble butter into dry ingredients, add egg yolk and sufficient milk to make a stiff dough. Knead until smooth. Shape into a roll and chill well, preferably overnight. Cut into thin slices and bake on buttered and floured baking sheet until golden brown on one side (Regulo 5), turn carefully, return to oven, switch off heat and finish drying in oven.

The pastry can be kept for quite a long time in refrigerator before baking.

ALMOND SLICES
MANDELSCHNITTEN

1½ oz. sugar	3 oz. chopped almonds
3 oz. butter	½ teaspoon flour
4½ oz. flour	Jam
3 egg whites	Melted chocolate
4 oz. granulated sugar	

Cream butter and sugar, add flour and work to a dough. Line a buttered baking sheet with this pastry (about one-eighth inch deep) and bake at Regulo 4 until top is lightly set (about five minutes). Meanwhile whisk egg whites until stiff, add sugar and almonds and stir over lowest possible flame in a thick saucepan until mixture is light pink. Remove from fire, stir in half teaspoon flour. Spread half-baked pastry with jam and then with the almond paste. Return pastry to oven (Regulo 6) until golden brown. Cut into squares while still hot, carefully dip one side into melted chocolate and set on waxed paper to dry.

ALMOND KISSES
MANDEL BUSSERL

Mix three ounces blanched and finely ground almonds with six ounces icing sugar. Care must be taken that almonds are perfectly dry before being ground and it is best to spread them on a flat dish after blanching to dry thoroughly. Gradually add a little egg white and one teaspoon lemon juice, beating all the time with a wooden spoon. Quantity of egg white required varies according to the size of the egg, but one medium-sized egg white is about sufficient for the above recipe. The mixture must not be wet but it should be 'workable'. Begin creaming the mixture as soon as this stage has been reached and continue creaming until the mixture is light and fluffy. Cover with a sieve and leave to stand for several hours—overnight if possible. Pipe small rounds of this mixture on to a very lightly buttered and floured baking sheet, leave to dry for one hour and bake at Regulo 2 (pre-heated oven) until lightly tinged with colour.

CHERRY STRUDEL
KIRSCHENSTRUDEL

Strudel pastry as described on   1½ *cups breadcrumbs*
  page 151   *Butter for frying*
FILLING: *Melted butter*
1 *lb. Morella cherries*   *Chopped walnuts*
¾ *cup sugar*   *Apricot jam*

Prepare *Strudel* pastry as described on page 151. Stone the cherries and sprinkle them with sugar. Fry breadcrumbs in butter. Sprinkle the fried breadcrumbs evenly over the pastry, then sprinkle cherries and chopped walnuts over half the surface only. Sprinkle with melted butter and dot with a little apricot jam. Tear off the rather thick rim which overhangs the table and start rolling the *Strudel* by lifting the cloth at the 'cherry' end. Roll up very carefully, like a Swiss roll, close up ends and place on buttered baking sheet, forming a horseshoe. Brush with melted butter and cover with greaseproof paper. Bake in a moderate oven (Regulo 4–4½) for about three-quarters of an hour, removing paper towards the end. Sprinkle with vanilla sugar.

HONEY BISCUITS
LEBZELT BAECKEREI

7 oz. sugar
2 eggs
Pinch each of powdered cin-
    namon, cloves, nutmeg and
    ginger

6 oz. honey
17 oz. flour
½ teaspoon bicarbonate of
    soda
egg for brushing over pastry

Sift together bicarbonate of soda and flour. Put sugar and eggs in a bowl and whisk until light and frothy. Add the warmed honey, spices and finally the flour. Mix well with a wooden spoon, pat into a round, cover and chill for three hours. After that time knead a little, then roll out the dough to about quarter-inch thickness. Cut into shapes with a biscuit cutter. Brush with egg and bake for about seven minutes on a well-buttered and floured baking sheet (Regulo 6). These biscuits harden slightly as they cool and soften again during storage.

APRICOT STRUDEL
MARILLENSTRUDEL

½ lb. puff pastry (see
    page 126)
Apricot jam

Apricots
Sugar
Egg for brushing over pastry

Roll out pastry and trim into a rectangle measuring about ten inches by six inches. Cut off two half-inch strips so that pastry now measures ten inches by five inches. Spread a little warmed apricot jam down centre of pastry to within one and a half inches of either edge. Cover centre strip with halved stoned apricots, sprinkle with sugar. Brush the uncovered side strips with egg, being careful that egg does not run down the cut edge. Fold one side of pastry over apricots, brush with egg, fold over other side. Make small strips from cut-off pieces of pastry and lay across fold. Secure ends. Brush over top of *Strudel*—but not over any of the cut edges—with egg. Set *Strudel* on a damped baking sheet. Light the oven at Regulo 7 and heat it for fifteen minutes before putting in *Strudel*. This gives the pastry time to 'settle' on the baking sheet. Bake until golden brown, lowering heat to Regulo 6 after about twenty minutes. When the *Strudel* is baked, dust it with icing sugar and return it to the oven for a few minutes with the heat switched off.

RAHMGUGLHUPF

Prepare a *Guglhupf* mould as described on page 164. Separate yolks and whites of three eggs. Sift together nine and a half ounces flour with a teaspoon baking powder, sift again. Whisk egg yolks with three ounces sugar, gradually add half pint cream and continue whisking until well blended and fluffy. Whisk egg whites until stiff, fold in two tablespoons sugar and whisk until smooth. Fold flour into egg yolks, etc., alternately with the stiffly beaten whites. Add a little grated lemon rind and about half a cup of washed and dried raisins. Bake for about three-quarters of an hour at Regulo 4½. Dust with vanilla sugar while still warm.

SOUR CREAM STRUDEL
MILCHRAHMSTRUDEL

Strudel pastry (see page 151)	½ *pint sour cream*
	¾ *cup breadcrumbs*
FILLING:	*Melted butter*
3½ *oz. butter*	¼ *pint milk*
3½ *oz. sugar*	*Grated lemon rind*
4 *eggs*	½ *cup raisins*

Prepare *Strudel* pastry as described on page 151. Wash and

dry the raisins, separate egg yolks and whites. Cream butter and sugar, add the egg yolks and lemon rind. Fold in the stiffly beaten egg whites alternately with the sour cream. Spread this filling over half the pastry, sprinkle with raisins and breadcrumbs. Brush the other half of the pastry with melted butter. Tear off the thick rim of pastry which overhangs the table. Roll up *Strudel* by lifting tablecloth at the filled end and roll as for Swiss roll. Set *Strudel* in a buttered deep baking dish, shaping the pastry into a 'snail'. Brush with melted butter.

Bake at Regulo 4½ until pastry begins to brown, pour the hot milk over it, turn up the heat to Regulo 5 and finish off baking. Serve with *Kanarienmilch* (see page 99).

MUERBE SCHNITTEN

5½ oz. butter	FILLING:
5½ oz. flour	3½ oz. ground walnuts, hazel
3 oz. sugar	nuts or almonds
1 egg	3½ oz. sugar
½ teaspoon baking powder	2 tablespoons milk
	Breadcrumbs

Sift together flour, sugar and baking powder. Add the egg and the butter and work to a smooth dough. Roll two-thirds of the dough into a strip about quarter-inch thick. Set on a buttered and floured baking sheet and bake for about eight minutes at Regulo 5. Meanwhile mix together ground walnuts, etc., sugar and milk and, if necessary, sufficient breadcrumbs to give a smooth spreading consistency. A few drops of rum improve the flavour. Roll remaining pastry into strips. Take half-baked pastry from the oven, spread with the nut mixture, arrange uncooked pastry strips in a criss-cross pattern over the filling and return to oven to complete baking. Serve cold, cut into slices and sprinkled thickly with vanilla sugar.

NUT ROLL
NUSS ROULADE

4 oz. ground almonds, walnuts or hazel nuts

3 eggs

Fine breadcrumbs or cake-crumbs

3½ oz. icing sugar

Whisk egg yolks with sugar until pale and creamy. Fold in ground nuts alternately with the stiffly beaten egg whites. Spread on a baking sheet previously buttered and spread with fine breadcrumbs or cakecrumbs. Bake for about a quarter of an hour at Regulo 4. Remove carefully and roll lightly over sugared paper. When cold unroll carefully and fill, roll up again. The traditional filling is sweetened whipped cream into which small wild strawberries and a dash of Kirsch have been folded. I have on occasion used the cream filling described on page 193 (see *Nut Gateau*) and strawberries and icecream, though very unorthodox, taste exceedingly good as a filling.

NUT BOATS
NUSS SCHIFFERL

2 oz. icing sugar

4 oz. butter or margarine

6 oz. flour

FILLING:

2 oz. ground nuts (walnuts or hazel nuts)

2 oz. icing sugar

A few drops rum

A little grated lemon or orange rind and juice

2 tablespoons lightly toasted biscuit or cakecrumbs

A little milk

Water icing

Crumble margarine (or butter) into flour and sugar and work to a smooth dough. Pat into a round and chill for thirty minutes. Roll out pastry and line small patty tins with it. Bake 'blind'. (Regulo 5.)

Mix together all ingredients for the filling and add sufficient milk to make a stiff paste. Fill pastry shells, smooth top with a knife dipped into hot water and cover with thin water icing.

JAM ENVELOPES
POLSTERZIPFEL

Cream cheese pastry   *Jam*
  (see page 154)   *Egg for brushing over pastry*

Roll out pastry to one-eighth-inch thickness, cut into two-inch squares (a zig-zag cutting wheel gives a nice finish). Place a blob of jam in the centre, fold over and press down edges so that pastry forms a triangle. Brush with egg and bake until golden brown (Regulo 5½). Sprinkle with vanilla sugar before serving.

In some parts of Austria this is also known as *Hasenohren* (Hare's ears).

REHRUECKEN

This is simply a good chocolate cake baked in a special cake tin, then covered with chocolate icing and spiked with strips of blanched almonds to imitate the larding on a haunch of venison (the literal translation of *Rehruecken*). The special cake tin is oblong and fluted in a particular way to denote the slices into which the cake is cut later on. It also has a 'dent' running down the centre, and after the cake has been covered with chocolate icing this dent is sometimes studded with halved glacé cherries or filled with redcurrant jelly to denote the 'backbone'. The cake can, of course, be baked in an ordinary cake tin and a good helping of sweetened whipped cream with each slice is optional. The recipe given below is for a very moist *Rehruekcen*, but any good chocolate cake mixture can be used—*Weiche Schoko-*

ladetorte, or *Schokoladetorte mit Mandeln* (see pages 203 and 201) or even *Sachertorte* (see page 199) when the cake becomes known as *Sacher Rehruecken.*

4½ oz. butter	4 eggs
4 oz. chocolate	Powdered cinnamon and
3 rounded tablespoons icing sugar	powdered cloves
1½ oz. good breadcrumbs	Rum

Separate egg yolks and whites. Break chocolate into small pieces and set in a warm place to melt. Cream butter and sugar, gradually add the melted (but not hot) chocolate and the egg yolks. Stir in a dash of rum. Fold in stiffly beaten egg whites alternately with the breadcrumbs, cloves and cinnamon. Bake in buttered and floured oblong cake tin (Regulo 4½). When cold spread with warmed redcurrant jelly, cover with chocolate icing (see page 199) and spike with strips of blanched almonds.

ROSE CAKES
ROSENKRAPFEN

Deep fat for frying	1 dessertspoon brandy, rum or
5 oz. flour	sherry
1½ oz. butter	1 oz. icing sugar
2 egg yolks	Pinch salt, jam, a little egg
1 dessertspoon top milk	white

Sift together salt, flour and sugar, sift again on to a board. Make a well in the centre, pour in the egg yolks, top milk and the brandy and work to a stiff paste with the butter. Cover with a cloth and leave for fifteen minutes. Roll out as thin as possible. Have ready three round pastry cutters, graded in size, and cut out an equal number of rounds in each size.

Place the two smaller rounds on top of the largest round, moistening the centre with a little egg white. Press down the centre of each 'rose' with a fingertip to make a small well. Make a few incisions round each rose to mark the petals. Have ready a small pan of smoking-hot fat and drop in the roses separately, petal side down. Turn when one side has browned, fry on other side. Drain on kitchen paper, then dust with vanilla sugar. Place a small blob of jam in centre of each 'rose'.

REDCURRANT FLAN
RIBISEL KUCHEN

Prepare a pastry with two ounces sugar, four ounces butter or margarine and six ounces flour, a few drops of lemon juice and line a buttered and floured rectangular flan tin with this. Bake 'blind'. When baked, but still hot, cover thickly with redcurrants, sprinkle with a little sugar. Whisk two egg whites until stiff, whisk in two ounces caster sugar, fold in another two ounces sugar. Pile whipped egg white over redcurrants and bake in cool oven until meringue top has set (Regulo 1). Cut into slices when cool.

SACHER GUGLHUPF

5 oz. butter	2 tablespoons rum
3 egg yolks	1 teaspoon baking powder
1 egg	10 oz. flour
5 oz. icing sugar	Jam, chocolate icing
About 5 tablespoons milk	(see page 199)

Butter a *Guglhupf* mould, sprinkle with flour, but do not cover with almonds as for other types of *Guglhupf*. Cream butter well, add the egg yolks and the whole egg alternately with the sugar. Beat well, then add the milk, rum and the flour (pre-

viously sifted with the baking powder), taking care that the
mixture does not curdle. Bake for about three-quarters of
an hour at Regulo 4½. When cold brush lightly with melted
jam, then cover with chocolate icing (see page 199).

CHOCOLATE KISSES
SCHOKOLADE BUSSERL

2 egg whites   5 oz. blanched almonds
2½ oz. icing sugar   Rice paper
3 oz. softened chocolate

Cut almonds into strips. Whip egg whites until stiff, fold in
half of the icing sugar, whisk again until smooth. Fold in
remaining sugar, softened chocolate (which must not be hot)
and almonds. Drop in spoonfuls on to rounds of rice paper,
leaving room to spread. Bake in very slow oven (Regulo 1–2)
until set and dry.

CHOCOLATE *FONDANT* BISCUITS
SCHOKOLADE FONDANT

7 oz. sugar   5 oz. ground toasted almonds
5 oz. butter   (not blanched)
5 oz. plain chocolate   1 tablespoon flour
                                    Glacé cherries for decoration

Break chocolate into small pieces and set to soften in a warm
place. Cream butter and sugar, add flour, almonds and the
softened chocolate.

Arrange small 'dabs' of the mixture on a buttered and
floured baking sheet, well apart. Flatten a little with a knife
and decorate with halved glacé cherries. Bake at Regulo 6.
Remove carefully from paper while still hot.

CHOCOLATE SLICES
SCHOKOLADESCHNITTEN

Cream three ounces butter with three ounces sugar. Add
four egg yolks gradually, as well as three ounces grated
chocolate. Fold in stiffly beaten whites of five eggs alternately
with two scant ounces fine breadcrumbs and one teaspoon
grated lemon rind. Spread about one and a half inches high
in a buttered and floured rectangular cake tin and bake at
Regulo 4½. Remove from tin while still warm, cool and cut into
slices. Cut slices through once and fill with chocolate cream as
for *Panamatorte* (see page 194) or *Dobos Torte* (see page 185).
Spread a little of the cream over the top as well and sprinkle
with chocolate vermicelli or grated chocolate.

SCHOKOLADEWURST

4 *oz. icing sugar*	3 *oz. grated chocolate*
1 *.egg*	1 *oz. mixed peel, chopped*
4 *oz. ground almonds*	1 *oz. blanched almonds cut*
(blanched)	*into strips*

Cream egg and sugar, add other ingredients. Shape into a
thick roll and dry very slowly in oven ('after baking' heat is
sufficient and the drying may be done in stages). Cut after
three days.

'RASCALS'
SPITZBUBEN

2 *oz. sugar*	5 *oz. flour*
3½ *oz. butter*	*Jam*
1 *egg*	

Sift together flour and sugar. Work to a smooth dough with

the butter and the egg. Roll out on a floured pastry board as thin as possible and cut into shapes with a biscuit cutter. Bake at Regulo 5 on a buttered and floured baking sheet until golden brown. Remove from baking sheet while still hot, sandwich two and two together when lightly cooled.

CHOCOLATE ROLL
SCHOKOLADE ROULADE

2 oz. chocolate	1 oz. ground almonds (not
3 eggs	blanched)
2 oz. sugar	Sweetened whipped cream

Break chocolate into small pieces and put in a warm place to soften. Add egg yolks and sugar and whisk until thick and fluffy. Fold in stiffly beaten egg whites, finally fold in ground almonds. Spread on a Swiss roll tin, lined with buttered greaseproof paper and bake (Regulo 5). Turn out on to sugared paper, remove paper sticking to pastry. Roll up lightly over sugared paper. When cold unroll, spread with sweetened whipped cream and roll up again. Dust with icing sugar.

CORNETS
STANITZL

2 eggs	¾ cup flour	¾ cup sugar

Whisk eggs with sugar until thick and fluffy. Fold in sifted flour. Drop in spoonfuls on to a well-buttered and floured baking sheet, leaving space for each round to spread. Flatten a little with a palette knife. Bake at Regulo 4 until pale golden brown. Remove from baking sheet while still hot and quickly twist into cornets (roll round the handle of a wooden cooking spoon and set cornets in a glass to keep the shape). The pastry hardens as it cools. Ideally they should be filled with sugared wild strawberries and cream, but sugared garden strawberries and a spoonful of good vanilla icecream are quite delicious too. For a more luxurious pastry, replace part of the flour with ground almonds or walnuts.

STRUDEL PASTE
STRUDELTEIG

There are *Strudeln* and *Strudeln*. Baked and boiled. Made with puff pastry and made with yeast. Savoury and sweet. But when the talk is of *Strudelteig* (the paste) it always means one thing only—a recipe of the type quoted below. Sometimes it may contain an egg, sometimes the egg yolk or the white only.

Strudel paste is not difficult to make. It requires a little practice, a 'feeling' for the paste as it were, and you are bound to get a few tears and holes now and then. Everybody does. In such cases I usually blame the flour, mumbling something about the necessity of *glattes Mehl* which is, of course, quite true. *Strudel* paste should be made with what is known in Austria as *glattes* flour. But it *can* be made—and I have made it many times—with ordinary plain flour.

THE PASTRY:
8 oz. *plain flour*
1 *teaspoon vinegar or lemon juice*

1 *heaped teaspoon butter*
About ¼ *pint warm water*
Pinch salt
Melted butter

Have everything nicely warmed—hands, liquid, pastry board. A wooden pastry board is much preferable to an enamelled one. If you have to use the latter, wipe it over with a cloth wrung out in hot water before starting. Sift flour and salt on to clean pastry board. Make a well in the centre, pour in vinegar or lemon juice. Cut butter into flour or crumble it with your fingers. Add enough warm water to make a soft dough and knead well until it 'blisters'. Bring it down on to the pastry board with a few smart slaps from time to time. Sprinkle dough with flour and cover with a warmed bowl—do not let the bowl touch the dough. Leave in a warm place for half an hour, renewing the covering bowl should it cool too rapidly. Prepare the filling during this time and set it aside. After half an hour the dough should be 'ripe' to start pulling operations. Cover a kitchen table with a clean cloth and sprinkle it with flour. If the kitchen table is not large enough, use the dining table (if larger) or halve the dough before you start pulling. Place the dough—floured side down—on the cloth and carefully roll out as far as it will go. Brush with a little melted butter, then slip your hands underneath the dough and pull it, using the balls of your thumbs, not the fingers, and always working from the middle, being careful not to tear the dough.

When the dough is pulled out to paper thinness, brush the pastry again with melted butter and leave to dry for ten to fifteen minutes.

BISCUITS I
TEEBAECKEREI I

4 oz. butter	*Pinch cinnamon*
6 oz. flour	*Pinch nutmeg*
6 oz. sugar	*Egg white for brushing over*
6 oz. ground almonds	*pastry*
(unblanched)	*Ground almonds for sprinkling*
1 oz. grated chocolate	*over pastry*
1 egg or 2 egg yolks	

Mix together the dry ingredients, cut butter into small pieces and crumble into dry ingredients. Work to a dough with the egg. Knead very well until quite smooth, roll out to one-eighth-inch thickness. Cut into shapes with a biscuit cutter, set on a floured buttered baking sheet, brush with egg white

and sprinkle with ground almonds. Bake at Regulo 5 until
nicely browned.

BISCUITS II
TEEBAECKEREI II

10 oz. flour
2½ oz. butter
3½ oz. sugar
1 egg

About 3 tablespoons cream
   or sour milk
A pinch of baking powder

Sift together dry ingredients, crumble butter into the mixture
and work to a smooth dough with the egg and the 'top milk'.
Knead well, roll out on a floured pastry board and leave overnight in a cool place. Cut into shapes with a biscuit cutter and
bake until golden brown (Regulo 5).

CREAM CHEESE SLICES
TOPFENSCHNITTEN

1 egg
1 oz. sugar

CREAM:
2 oz. butter
2 oz. sugar
1 egg yolk

1 oz. ground walnuts or
   almonds
1 teaspoon flour

1 teaspoon grated lemon rind
About 2½ oz. cream cheese
Toasted ground almonds

Whisk together egg and sugar over steam until thick, remove
from fire and whisk until cool. Fold in ground walnuts or
almonds and flour. Spread on a buttered and floured baking
sheet and bake at Regulo 5½. Cut into slices and remove from
baking sheet while still hot.

Cream butter and sugar, add the egg yolk and the cream
cheese, beat in the grated lemon rind. Spread this cream

thickly over the pastry and sprinkle toasted ground almonds over the top.

PUFF PASTRY MADE WITH CREAM CHEESE
TOPFENBLAETTERTEIG

¼ lb. flour   ¼ lb. cream cheese
¼ lb. butter

Sift flour on to pastry board. Cut butter into small pieces, crumble cream cheese and butter into flour, handling dough as lightly as possible. Pat dough into a round and chill well before using as required (chill overnight if possible). You can also use it for sausage rolls or—cut into strips, brushed with egg white, sprinkled with coarse salt, paprika and caraway seeds and baked—as a cocktail savoury. An egg yolk may be added to the basic recipe quoted above.

CREAM CHEESE CRESCENTS
TOPFENKIPFERL

Pastry as above.

FILLING:
3 oz. blanched almonds   1 oz. sugar
2 egg whites   Egg yolk for brushing over
Juice and rind of ½ lemon   pastry

Grate almonds finely. Whip egg whites until stiff, whisk in the sugar. Fold in almonds, lemon juice and rind. Roll out pastry to one-eighth-inch thickness, cut into squares. Place a little of the filling in the centre of each square, fold over pastry, roll up and shape into a crescent. Brush with egg yolk and bake until golden brown (Regulo 5).

VANILLA CRESCENTS
VANILLEKIPFERL

1 oz. ground almonds	3 oz. butter
(unblanched)	4 oz. flour
2 oz. sugar	Vanilla sugar

Sift together flour and sugar. Add ground almonds. Cut butter into small pieces and crumble into dry ingredients. Knead into a firm paste. Take small pieces of the dough, roll between your hands, bend into crescents. Bake on a buttered and floured baking sheet at Regulo 5 until dark golden brown, roll in vanilla sugar (icing sugar in which a vanilla pod has been kept) while still hot.

ZAUNERSTOLLEN

These should really be made with *Zauner Oblaten* (wafers made specially by the House of Zauner in Ischl), but ordinary ice wafers can be used, provided they are dry and not soggy.

¼ pint cream	3 oz. hazel nuts
3 oz. grated chocolate	3 oz. ice wafers
Chocolate icing (see page 199)	

Place hazel nuts on a baking sheet and put them in a hot oven for a few minutes until skins come off easily. Put hazel nuts in a clean towel, rub off skins and then grind hazel nuts, or chop them finely. Put chocolate in a saucepan together with the cream and bring slowly to the boil, stirring constantly. Remove from fire, whisk until cool. Add hazel nuts and crumbled ice wafers. Pour into an oblong cake tin lined with buttered greaseproof paper and leave in a cold place until well set. Turn out of mould, remove paper and ice with chocolate icing. Cut with a hot knife. (It is best left for a day or even two before cutting.)

MORELLA CHERRY CAKE
WEICHSELKUCHEN

2 oz. butter
2 oz. sugar
2 oz. ground almonds
  (unblanched)
1 oz. fine breadcrumbs

2 eggs
A little lemon juice, cinnamon,
  pinch nutmeg
1 cup stoned morella cherries

Separate egg yolks and whites. Cream butter with one ounce
sugar, add yolks gradually. Whisk egg whites until stiff, whisk
in remaining sugar. Fold stiffly beaten egg whites into creamed
butter, alternately with ground almonds and breadcrumbs.
Fold in morella cherries, lemon juice, cinnamon and nutmeg.
Bake in a buttered and floured cake tin at Regulo 4 for about
thirty-five minutes.

WIDOW'S KISSES
WITWENKUESSE

2 egg whites
2½ oz. sugar
2½ oz. chopped nuts

1½ oz. chopped mixed peel
Rice paper

Whisk egg whites and sugar over steam until thick, remove
from fire, whisk until cold. Fold in chopped nuts (walnuts,
hazel nuts or almonds or a mixture of all three), chopped mixed
peel. Arrange in small heaps on rounds of rice paper and bake
at Regulo ½ until lightly tinged with colour.

GIPSY SLICES
ZIGEUNERSCHNITTEN

These are filled with the most luscious of all cream fillings—

Pariser Creme. Cream is an absolute necessity and it's no good trying any substitute. It just doesn't work.

2 *eggs*	1 *oz. chocolate*
2 *oz. sugar*	½ *oz. butter*
2 *oz. flour*	

Break chocolate into small pieces, place in a bowl, together with the butter and set to soften in a warm place. Put eggs and sugar in a bowl and whisk over steam until thick, remove from fire and whisk until cool. Lightly fold in flour and finally the softened butter and chocolate. Spread about half-inch thick on buttered greaseproof paper, place on a baking sheet and bake at Regulo 6. Remove paper while still hot. Cut into slices, cut through each slice once and fill with:

PARISER CREME:

¼ *pint cream*	2 *oz. grated chocolate*

Put grated chocolate in a thick saucepan, add cream and bring to boil slowly, stirring constantly. Leave to rise once, remove from fire and stir until cool. Chill well. Whisk lightly, until it will just hold its shape. Chill again before using.

CINNAMON STARS
ZIMTSTERNE

9 *oz. sugar*	½ *egg white*
9 *oz. blanched almonds (ground)*	3½ *oz. icing sugar*
¼ *oz. cinnamon*	*Lemon juice*
3 *tablespoons water*	

Sift together sugar and cinnamon. Add ground almonds and mix together. Make a little well in centre and add the water and a little egg white (about half an egg white). Knead well to a firm dough. Roll out on a sugared (not floured) pastry board to quarter-inch thickness and cut into stars with a pastry cutter. Place on a sugared pastry sheet and dry at lowest possible heat in oven (heat after oven has been turned off is sufficient), then bake at Regulo 2 until deep golden brown. Mix the icing sugar with sufficient lemon juice to give a thick consistency and spread over stars. Leave to dry.

CHEESE BISCUITS
KAESEBAECKEREI

4½ oz. grated cheese
2 oz. butter
4½ oz. flour

1 egg yolk
A few walnuts or hazel nuts
     for decoration

Work all the ingredients to a stiff paste, roll out and cut into shapes. Brush with a little egg white or milk and place a nut in centre of each biscuit. Bake until golden brown (Regulo 5). Alternately, only decorate half the biscuits with nuts and when cool, sandwich two and two together with a paste made of creamed butter to which one or two finely scraped anchovies have been added.

HAM BISCUITS
SCHINKENBAECKEREI

Sift together eleven ounces flour with a pinch salt. Crumble seven ounces butter or margarine into the flour, add two hard-boiled egg yolks and enough 'top milk' to give a stiff paste (about one-eighth pint). Knead well, pat into a round and chill for one hour. Roll out to one-eighth-inch thickness, brush with egg or egg yolk, sprinkle with chopped ham. Fold sides to middle, roll out pastry as before. Brush again with egg, sprinkle again with chopped ham, fold sides to middle and roll out. Leave for twenty minutes. Roll out to one-eighth-inch thickness, brush with egg, sprinkle with coarse salt and caraway seeds and leave for one to two hours. Cut into strips or shapes and bake in hot oven until golden brown (Regulo 6).

YEAST

There is nothing complicated about cooking with yeast. Recipes may vary, but the basic fundamentals remain the same: A warm, slightly steamy kitchen, as free of draughts as possible. A comfortably warm place for the dough to rise in. Yeast dies if the heat is too great and, failing all else, set the bowl over steam. The necessity of 'proving' the yeast: It is mixed with a little sugar, flour and tepid milk and set in a warm place. This is done for two reasons. Firstly to prove that the yeast is still 'live'—it will come up in a froth of small bubbles if this is the case. If it doesn't, you will not have wasted your other ingredients. Secondly, yeast thus dissolved is more evenly distributed throughout the dough.

Yeast dough is quite tough, though it feels very soft to the touch. It does not require extra-special handling, but it is grateful for being worked on a wooden pastry board. Although the quantities for milk are stated, these vary sometimes, according to the flour.

BUCHTELN

14 oz. flour
Pinch salt
About ⅜ pint milk
3 egg yolks (or 1 egg and
  1 egg yolk)
2 oz. sugar

3½ oz. butter
Jam
Melted butter or margarine
  for brushing over buns
½ oz. yeast
Grated lemon rind

Set the three and a half ounces butter to melt in a warm place. Cream yeast with a teaspoon of the sugar and a pinch of flour. Heat milk a little, it should only be tepid. Stir half a cup of the milk into the creamed yeast and set to prove in a warm place. Sift flour and salt into a warmed mixing bowl. Put egg yolks (or egg and egg yolk), remaining sugar, milk and melted butter in a bowl and whisk until well blended. Make a well in centre of flour and stir egg, milk, etc., into flour, add lemon rind and yeast. Beat well with a wooden spoon until dough leaves sides of spoon and bowl clean. Dust with a little flour and cover with a cloth. Leave to rise for about one hour. Butter and lightly flour a cake tin or deep baking dish. Roll out pastry to about quarter-inch thickness (floured pastry board) and cut into two-and-a-half-inch squares. Place a good dab of jam in centre of each square and fold together (this is best done by picking up the four corners, pinching them well together in the middle so that the jam is completely enclosed). Pack the small buns next to each other—they should touch closely—in the cake tin after brushing each bun carefully with melted butter or margarine. (The 'pinched-together' edges should be at the bottom of the tin.) One good way of moistening the buns with melted butter is to dip them very lightly into the melted butter and then spread the butter lightly all over the bun. Brush a little melted butter over the top of the buns, cover tin with a cloth and leave to rise for half an hour. Bake at Regulo 5 until nicely browned. Take out of cake tin and leave to cool on a sieve. Separate buns when cold and sprinkle liberally with icing sugar.

FASCHINGSKRAPFEN

About ⅛ pint of cream
8 oz. flour
½ oz. yeast
1 teaspoon sugar
1 dessertspoon rum
1 teaspoon lemon juice
1 teaspoon orange juice

1 teaspoon grated orange or
    lemon rind
1 oz. sugar
Pinch salt
3 egg yolks
2 oz. melted butter
Apricot jam

Fat for frying

Respectable *Faschingskrapfen* are noted for the white band which runs right round their plump middles. Apart from that, they should be deep golden brown, nicely rounded and rather well-proportioned. Here then are my own special hints—and it might be as well to say at this point that many a *Krapfen* which lacked some or all of the above qualifications was devoured with prodigious speed in my kitchen!

(1) Have everything nicely warmed—flour, mixing bowl, pastry board, hands, etc., and be careful to shut out all draughts. This is more important with doughnuts than with any other type of yeast pastry.

(2) You may prefer to let dough rise only once, i.e., when the *Krapfen* are already cut out, rather than letting it rise twice, i.e., before rolling it out and then when the doughnuts have been stamped into rounds. Personally I prefer the latter method. It is of course a matter of personal preference, but if you decide to let the *Krapfen* rise only once you must allow more time for this.

(3) Do not expect the dough to be firm—it should be very soft indeed and only just manageable. Press it out with your knuckles rather than rolling it and you will at the same time dispel any small air bubbles which would swell with the frying and spoil the appearance of the finished product. Some cooks even advise a few smart slaps with the hand against the dough for that reason—for which I have so far lacked the courage, though it sounds reasonable enough.

(4) Whenever you handle the doughnuts or the dough itself, turn them upside down, e.g., when you set the doughnuts on the tray to rise, when you put them in the hot fat, etc.

(5) Brush off all flour before putting doughnuts in the fat.

(6) In Vienna one could buy special *Krapfenschmalz* to fry doughnuts in. Pure lard (the emphasis is on pure) is best after that, though it does brown the doughnuts rather fast, or really good quality cooking fat. A small piece of bees-wax added to either improves the appearance.

(7) Whether rolling out the dough or 'pressing it out' with

your knuckles, lift dough very carefully from time to time so that it 'runs' towards the centre—this gives a better shape to the finished product.

(8) Do not cut the *Krapfen* too small—about two and a half inches across is best.

(9) The doughnuts should literally 'swim' in the fat, which means not only that the fat must be deep enough (about two inches) but also that the *Krapfen* must have risen sufficiently so that they are light enough to float.

(10) Fry doughnuts on one side in a covered frying pan, turn them and fry on the other side with the lid off.

METHOD:

Cream yeast with one teaspoon sugar, add a little of the cream (tepid), sprinkle in a pinch of the flour and set in a warm place to 'prove'. When it has risen and bubbles, it is ready for use. Meanwhile whisk together egg yolks and sugar, gradually add the cream, lemon juice, orange juice, lemon rind, rum and salt. Fold in flour, add yeast and finally the melted butter. Beat well with a wooden spoon until dough leaves sides of bowl clean. Sprinkle with a little flour, cover with a cloth and leave in a warm place until about doubled in bulk (about one hour). Turn out on to a floured pastry board, cool a little, knead once so that dough is perfectly smooth. Carefully roll out with a rolling pin or press out with your knuckles to about one-eighth-inch thickness. Mark half the dough into rounds, cut other half into rounds (about two and a half inches across). Place a little firm apricot jam in centre of marked rounds, cover with cut-out rounds, placing them on the jam upside down (i.e. side that was upper-most should cover jam). Press down edges, and with a smaller circular cutter stamp into rounds. Set on a tray (or baking sheet) covered with a clean cloth sprinkled with flour. Cover lightly with a warmed floured cloth and leave to rise in a warm place.

Use up left-over dough in the same way, adding a little

milk if it has become too dry. Test doughnuts very lightly with your fingers and when they feel 'downy' they are ready for frying. Test temperature of fat by sprinkling in a drop of water—if it sizzles properly, fat is the right temperature (the damped handle of a wooden cooking spoon dipped into the fat is another good test). Put doughnuts upside down in the hot fat. Cover frying pan with a lid and fry until one side of doughnuts is deep golden brown.

Lift off lid, turn doughnuts over on other side (sometimes they conveniently turn themselves when one side is fried) and finish frying on other side with the lid off. Drain on paper and dust liberally with icing sugar.

GUGLHUPF AUS GERMTEIG I
(For other *Guglhupf* recipes see pages 130, 142 and 147)

Ideally this should be baked in a real *Guglhupf* form (a type of fluted savarin tin) which can on occasion be found in shops specialising in Continental kitchen ware. You can of course use an ordinary savarin tin instead, but a *Guglhupf* form is worth hunting for. I would even venture to say it's worth bringing one back from the Continent—a *Guglhupf* really does taste better when baked in its proper 'setting'. This is not an optical illusion but a matter of simple arithmetic: fluting means an increased surface over which to sprinkle the blanched almonds, a very essential part of this delectable cake! On the Continent *Guglhupf* forms are generally available in copper, in aluminium, in enamel and more recently also in fireproof glass, but ask any Viennese housewife and she will plump straight for one made in fireproof pottery—and after all, she should know!

⅔ oz. yeast
3 egg yolks
5½ oz. butter (*see note below*)
4 oz. sugar
1 lb. flour

½ pint milk
Grated lemon rind
½ cup washed and dried
   raisins
½ cup blanched almonds

A number of cooks (and very good ones at that) insist that a mixture of half butter and half pure lard gives a better consistency and flavour to their *Guglhupf*. One cook of my acquaintance swears to this day that the only way to get a really satisfactory result is to use a third of butter, one-third of good margarine and one-third of pure lard. It is greatly a matter of personal taste. You can use half butter and half margarine. Or half butter and half lard (if you are sure of the quality of the lard). Or all margarine. Or half margarine and half lard. But *never* all lard. And whatever happens, beg, borrow or steal enough butter for the cake tin—it does made all the difference!

Cream yeast with half an ounce sugar, warm the milk until it is tepid and add a little to the creamed yeast. Stand in a warm place to 'prove'. Butter cake tin well, sprinkle with blanched almonds (cut into thin strips) and dust lightly with flour. (Ground almonds instead of the flour sprinkled over the cake tin greatly enhance the flavour.) Cream the butter and the sugar, gradually add the egg yolks. Add a little of the flour, then the 'proved' yeast and the remainder of the flour alternately with the milk. Beat well either with the hand or with a wooden spoon until dough leaves spoon and sides of bowl clean. Add raisins and a little grated lemon rind. Arrange dough in cake tin, cover with a cloth and leave to rise in a warm place. The cake tin should be about three-quarters filled and the cake left to rise until dough comes to within half an inch of rim of cake tin. Put cake in a hot oven (Regulo 7), lower heat after about six minutes to Regulo 6 and a little later to Regulo 4½–5. Cover top of cake with buttered greaseproof paper if it gets browned too quickly during baking. When baked turn carefully out of tin, leave to cool a little, then sprinkle thickly with vanilla sugar (icing sugar in which a vanilla pod has been kept).

GUGLHUPF AUS GERMTEIG II

This is sometimes described as 'French *Guglhupf*' in Vienna and is a slightly quicker method.

9 oz. flour
4 oz. butter
½ cup blanched almonds
½ cup washed and dried
   raisins

½ cup milk
3 eggs
2 tablespoons sugar
½ oz. fresh yeast
Grated lemon rind

Sift flour into a warmed bowl. Mix yeast with a little of the sugar and the tepid milk. Make a well in centre of flour and pour in the yeast mixture. Sprinkle with a little flour, cover with a cloth and set in a warm place to 'prove'. Butter a *Guglhupf* mould (or savarin tin). Sprinkle with blanched almonds cut into strips, then sprinkle with flour. Set butter to melt in a warm place. When the yeast mixture begins to bubble, mix yeast into remainder of flour, add remaining sugar and lightly beaten eggs. Beat well with a wooden spoon (or with the hand), gradually adding the melted butter which must not be hot. Beat until mixture leaves spoon and sides of bowl clean. Stir in the raisins and the grated lemon rind. Arrange mixture in prepared cake tin which should be about two-thirds full. Set in a warm place to rise. When mixture has risen to within half an inch of top of cake tin put the cake in a hot oven (Regulo 7), turn down heat to Regulo 5 (and later 4½) after five minutes, without opening oven door. Bake for about forty minutes in all—you may have to cover top of cake with buttered greaseproof paper in case this browns too quickly. Dust with icing sugar while cake is still warm.

RAISIN OR SULTANA BREAD
MILCHBROT

11 oz. flour
2 oz. sugar
½ oz. yeast
1½ oz. butter (melted)
¼ pint milk
1 egg

Pinch salt
Grated lemon rind
½ cup washed and dried
   raisins or sultanas
Egg for brushing over pastry

Cream yeast with one teaspoon sugar, add half cup tepid milk. Sprinkle with a little flour and set in a warm place to prove. Sift remaining flour and sugar into a warmed bowl, add egg, melted butter, salt, grated lemon rind and dissolved yeast. Gradually add the milk. Beat well with a wooden spoon until dough is smooth and shiny and leaves sides of the bowl clean. Sprinkle with a little flour and put in a warm place to rise (about half an hour). Tip contents of bowl on to a floured pastry board, add the sultanas and divide dough into three equal parts. Shape into long rolls, plait into a loaf. Put the loaf on a buttered and floured baking dish or cake tin, cover with a cloth and leave to rise in a warm place (about twenty minutes). Brush with egg and bake, first at Regulo 7 for about six minutes, lowering the heat gradually and finish baking at Regulo 4½.

Egg yolk only may be used for this recipe in which case the quantity of milk has to be slightly increased. Top of sultana loaf may be sprinkled with sugar before or after baking. To be eaten sliced, with butter and jam or honey.

PLAITED COFFEE LOAF
KAFFEESTRIEZEL

14 oz. flour	1 egg and 1 egg yolk
½ oz. yeast	(or 1 large egg)
1 teaspoon flour	2–3 oz. raisins
½ teaspoon sugar	½ cup blanched almonds
2 oz. melted butter	Egg and sugar for brushing
¼ pint milk	over cake
2½ oz. sugar	

Cream yeast with half teaspoon sugar, add one teaspoon flour and one-eighth pint tepid milk and set in a warm place to prove. Sift seven ounces flour into a warmed bowl. Make a well in centre and add the yeast and the remaining milk. Work dough with a wooden spoon or with your hand until it is perfectly smooth. Sprinkle with a little flour, set in a warm place to rise (about twenty minutes).

Whisk egg (or egg and egg yolk) with sugar, gradually add one-eighth pint milk and finally the remaining flour and melted butter. Mix together the two kinds of dough and work well until dough begins to blister. Add the washed and dried raisins, sprinkle with a little flour and leave to rise again (about one hour). Sprinkle pastry board with flour, divide dough into three equal parts (it will be very soft and has to be handled rather carefully). Shape each part into a roll and then plait rolls into a loaf. Carefully set loaf in a buttered and floured baking tin and put in a warm place to rise. Brush loaf with egg in which a little sugar has been dissolved and sprinkle with blanched almonds cut into strips. Bake at Regulo 4½ for about thirty-five to forty minutes.

NUT CRESCENTS
NUSSBEUGEL

8 oz. flour	1½ oz. sugar
4 oz. butter or margarine	½ oz. yeast
Pinch salt	About ¼ cup milk

FILLING:

3½ oz. ground walnuts	A little rum
2½ oz. biscuit or cake crumbs or grated honeycake	Grated lemon rind
	Cinnamon
¼ pint water	Egg for brushing over pastry
2 oz. sugar	

Cream yeast with a pinch sugar, add tepid milk and set to prove in a warm place. Sift together remaining sugar, pinch of salt and flour. Make a little well in the centre and pour in the yeast. Cut the butter or margarine into the flour and mix everything to a smooth dough. Divide pastry into two or three equal lumps and knead each one separately until very smooth. Cover with a cloth and leave for ten to fifteen minutes (do not set to rise). Shape each piece into a roll and cut off small chunks, about half an inch thick. Flatten these with a rolling pin and spread with filling. Fold over pastry, press together edges and shape into small crescents. Set on a buttered and floured baking sheet and spread with egg yolk. Wait for egg yolk to dry, then brush with egg white. Place in hot oven (Regulo 7½), lower heat to 6 about four minutes later and bake until golden brown. Crescents will have a 'marbled' finish.

For the filling dissolve sugar in water and bring to boil. Mix together walnuts and crumbs, add lemon rind, cinnamon and a dash of rum. Pour boiling sugar solution over crumbs, etc., and stir well. Leave to cool before using.

POPPYSEED CRESCENTS
MOHNBEUGEL

Pastry as for Nut Crescents
  (see above)
⅛ *pint water*
¼ *pint ground poppy seeds*
2 *oz. sugar*

Rum
Grated lemon rind
Cinnamon
Egg for brushing over
  pastry

Dissolve sugar in water, bring to boil and mix with ground poppy seeds. Add rum, grated lemon rind and cinnamon and leave to cool. Fill and bake crescents as described above for Nut Crescents. Cake or biscuit crumbs (or grated honey-cake) may partly replace the poppy seeds and honey may be used instead of sugar for sweetening.

NUSSPOTITZE

5 oz. butter
2½ oz. sugar
3 egg yolks
1 oz. yeast

¼ pint milk
10 oz. flour
A little grated lemon rind

FILLING:
1 lb. walnuts
6 oz. sugar
¼ pint rum
⅜ pint honey

2 tablespoons raisins
A little grated lemon rind
Lemon juice, cinnamon
⅛ pint cream

Butter and flour a savarin tin. Cream yeast with a little of the sugar, add tepid milk. Add a pinch of flour and set to prove in a warm place. Cream butter and sugar, add yolks. Add flour alternately with yeast and milk. Beat well with a wooden spoon until dough comes away clean from the spoon. Sprinkle pastry board with flour, spread dough over pastry board, cover with the filling, roll up and set in savarin tin. Put in a warm place, cover with a cloth and leave to rise for about forty minutes. Bake at Regulo 5 for about one hour.

For the filling put all ingredients (except honey and rum) in a bowl. Heat the honey and stir into other ingredients, add the rum.

NUT STRUDEL MADE WITH YEAST
NUSS STRUDEL

7 oz. flour
¾ gill milk
Pinch salt
1 oz. sugar
1 egg
Grated lemon rind

2 oz. melted butter
½ oz. yeast
½ oz. flour
1 teaspoon sugar
Egg for brushing over pastry

FILLING: 1 *tablespoon butter*
3 oz. *ground walnuts*   *A little rum*
2 oz. *cake or biscuit crumbs*   *Grated lemon rind*
1 oz. *sugar*   *Cinnamon*
Scant ¼ pint milk

Cream yeast with one teaspoon sugar, add a little of the milk (tepid) and half an ounce flour. Set to prove in a warm place. Sift salt, flour and sugar into a warmed mixing bowl, add lemon rind, egg, remainder of milk and dissolved yeast. Finally add the melted butter. Beat well with a wooden spoon until dough leaves sides of bowl clean. Sprinkle with a little flour, cover with a cloth and set to rise in a warm place (one hour). Tip dough on to floured pastry board, knead very lightly so that dough is perfectly smooth, sprinkle with a little flour and roll out to about one-eighth-inch thickness. Spread with filling, roll up as for Swiss roll. Bend into a horseshoe and set on a buttered and floured baking sheet. Cover with a cloth and leave to rise in a warm place for half an hour. Brush with egg and bake at Regulo 5.

Filling: dissolve sugar and butter in milk, bring to boil and pour over walnuts and crumbs. Mix well, add rum, cinnamon, lemon rind and leave to cool before using.

POPPYSEED STRUDEL MADE WITH YEAST
MOHNSTRUDEL

Pastry as for Nut Strudel   *Grated lemon rind*
   (see above)   1 *tablespoon washed and*
Egg for brushing over pastry   *dried raisins*
FILLING: 1 oz. *butter*
4 oz. *ground poppy seeds*   2 oz. *sugar*
Scant ¼ pint milk   *Cinnamon*

Prepare in exactly the same way as *Nut Strudel*. For the filling cook ground poppy seeds in milk until thick. Add butter and sugar and remove from fire. Stir well, adding grated lemon rind and a sprinkling of cinnamon at the same time. Finally stir in the raisins. Cool before using.

PLUM CAKE MADE WITH YEAST
ZWETSCHKENKUCHEN

5 oz. flour	Pinch salt
¼ oz. yeast	Grated lemon rind
1 oz. sugar	⅜ pint milk
2 oz. melted butter	Plums
1 egg yolk	
TO SPRINKLE OVER CAKE:	1 oz. sugar
2½ oz. flour	1 oz. blanched ground almonds
1 oz. butter	A little milk or egg white

Cream yeast with a little (about half a cup) of the milk and a pinch of sugar and flour. Set in a warm place to prove. Sift remaining flour with sugar and salt into a warmed mixing bowl, make a well in centre and drop in the egg yolk. Add the milk, grated lemon rind, dissolved yeast, melted butter, and beat well with a wooden spoon until dough is smooth and shiny. Spread on a buttered and floured baking sheet, cover thickly with halved plums (skin side downwards and set to rise in a warm place under a cloth. Meanwhile sift two and a half ounces flour and one ounce sugar into a bowl, add the ground almonds and crumble butter into this. Add a few drops milk (or egg white) and when plum cake has well risen (after about forty-five minutes), sprinkle this mixture thickly over plums. Bake at Regulo 5½, lowering heat towards end of baking time. Sprinkle thickly with sugar when cooled a little.

PUFF PASTRY MADE WITH YEAST I
GERMBUTTERTEIG I

4 oz. butter
8 oz. flour
1 oz. yeast (scant)
½ oz. sugar
1 egg yolk

About half cup milk
1 teaspoon flour for mixing
  yeast
Pinch salt

Sift flour and salt and divide into two equal parts of four ounces each. Cut butter into four ounces flour, knead a little, shape into a brick and chill.

Cream yeast with sugar, add lukewarm milk and one teaspoon flour and put in a warm place to 'prove'. Sift remaining flour into a warmed bowl, make a little well in centre and drop in the egg yolk. When the yeast begins to throw light bubbles, stir egg yolk into flour, add yeast mixture and knead to a smooth dough. (A little more lukewarm milk may have to be added—this depends entirely on the size of the egg yolk and quality of flour.) Pat yeast dough into a round, cover with a cloth and set to rise for about fifteen minutes in a warm place. After that time place dough on a floured pastry board and leave to cool for a little. Roll out yeast dough to about three times the size of the butter brick. Place butter brick in centre, fold yeast dough over it. Beat with a rolling pin, then roll out to original size. Fold dough into three again, beat with rolling pin, then roll out. Repeat this once more, place pastry in a cool place for half an hour before using.

PUFF PASTRY MADE WITH YEAST II
GERMBUTTERTEIG II

5 oz. flour
Pinch salt
⅓ oz. yeast
1 oz. melted butter
½ oz. sugar
1 large egg yolk

½ cup milk
1 teaspoon flour for mixing
  yeast
3 oz. butter
1 oz. flour

Cut three ounces butter into one ounce flour, shape into a brick and chill.

Cream yeast with sugar, add lukewarm milk and one teaspoon flour and set in a warm place to 'prove'. Sift flour with salt, make a well in centre and drop in the egg yolk. When the yeast begins to 'bubble', add it to the flour, mix well and stir in the melted butter. Knead well until dough is very smooth. Sprinkle with a little flour, cover with a cloth and leave for a quarter of an hour. After that time, knead dough for half a minute so that it is really smooth, then roll out on a floured pastry board to about three times the size of the butter brick (dough should be slightly thicker towards the centre). Place chilled butter brick in centre, fold sides of yeast pastry over butter brick and beat well with a rolling pin. Roll out pastry to a strip, fold both sides to middle, then fold pastry in half—rather like closing a book. Cover pastry with a cloth and leave in a cool place for half an hour. Repeat rolling and folding process—first folding pastry into three parts, rolling it out, then folding it into four parts and finally folding it over again. Leave dough for fifteen minutes (longer if possible) in a cool place, then use as required.

CROISSANTS
BUTTERKIPFERL

Puff pastry made with yeast II   Egg yolk for brushing over
(page 172)   pastry

Roll out pastry to a square about one-eighth-inch thick. Cut into squares first, then divide squares into triangles. Roll into crescents and set on a buttered and floured baking sheet to rise. When well risen brush over with egg yolk and bake in hot oven until golden brown (Regulo 5½).

There are, of course, various ways of embellishing these croissants. You may like to spread a little icing over them while they are still warm or sprinkle them with chopped walnuts or almonds before baking. You can fill them with jam or raisins grated nuts and chocolate, or you might like to try the following:

BUTTERKIPFERL AU CHEVALIER

Puff pastry made with yeast II   *2 oz. ground hazelnuts*
   (page 172)   *A little grated lemon rind*
2 egg whites   *Cinnamon*
3 oz. icing sugar   *Egg for brushing over pastry*

Roll out pastry to a square about one-eighth-inch thick. Cut into squares. Whisk egg whites until stiff, whisk in the sugar, then fold in ground hazel nuts and lemon rind and cinnamon. Place a little of the filling in centre of each square, roll up pastry and shape into crescents. Secure each little 'flap' with a touch of egg. Set crescents on a buttered and floured baking sheet to rise. When doubled in size, brush with egg and bake in hot oven (Regulo 5). Sprinkle with icing sugar when still warm.

MARZIPAN CRESCENTS
MARZIPAN KIPFERL

Puff pastry made with   *2 oz. sugar*
   yeast II (page 172)   *I egg*
¼ lb. blanched almonds   *Egg yolk for brushing over*
   (ground)   *pastry*

Mix together almonds and sugar, work to a smooth paste with the egg. Prepare pastry as described on page 172. Roll out to one-eighth-inch thickness and cut into squares. Spread with the almond paste to within one-eighth-inch of the edge, roll up and shape into a crescent. Set on a buttered and floured baking sheet, cover with a cloth and set in a warm place to rise. When risen to about double the original size, brush with egg yolk and bake at Regulo 5 until golden brown.

HAZEL NUT ROLLS
HASELNUSS ROLLEN

(About 25 small rolls)

Puff pastry made with yeast I
  (page 172)
5 oz. ground hazel nuts
1 dessertspoon honey
1 tablespoon sugar

½ oz grated chocolate
1 egg white
Cinnamon, grated lemon rind
Egg yolk for brushing over
  pastry

Set aside about half an ounce ground hazel nuts for sprinkling over pastry. Mix together all other ingredients and work well with a wooden spoon. A little more honey or a few drops milk may have to be added if egg white is too small. Roll out the pastry to about one-eighth-inch thickness, cut into squares. Place a little of the hazel nut mixture down the centre of each square, shape into small rolls (brush one side of pastry with egg yolk before folding over second half). Place rolls on a buttered and floured baking sheet and set in a warm place to rise. When risen to about twice their original size, brush with egg yolk, sprinkle with ground hazel nuts and bake in hot oven until golden brown (Regulo 6).

RING CAKE
KRANZKUCHEN

Puff pastry made with
  yeast II (page 172)
1 tablespoon melted butter
1 oz. ground or chopped
  almonds (not blanched)
½ cup washed and dried
  raisins

1 oz. grated chocolate
About 1 tablespoon cake or
  biscuit crumbs
Rum
Icing sugar
Cinnamon
Egg for brushing over pastry

Roll out pastry into a rectangular piece, about one-eighth-inch thick. Mix together ground or chopped almonds, raisins, grated chocolate, crumbs and about one tablespoon sugar. Sprinkle over rolled-out pastry, then sprinkle with rum, a little cinnamon and finally with the melted butter. Roll up as for Swiss roll. Placing the folded-over edge underneath, twist into a round and set in a buttered and floured cake tin. Secure ends well so that the filling stays sealed in during the baking. Make a few incisions along the top. Cover with a cloth and set in a warm place to rise. When risen to about twice its original size brush with egg and place in hot oven (Regulo 5½). Bake until deep golden brown, lowering heat towards the end of the baking time (Regulo 4½). Remove from oven, mix a little icing sugar with a few drops rum and spread over top of cake while still warm but not hot.

NUT RING
NUSSKRANZ

*Puff pastry made with
    yeast II (page 172)*
3-4 *oz. ground walnuts*
2 *oz. biscuit crumbs or
    grated honeycake*

Grated lemon rind
Cinnamon
A little cream
1 *tablespoon sugar*
Egg for brushing over pastry

Mix together ground walnuts, biscuit crumbs, grated lemon rind, a little cinnamon, sugar (or honey) and sufficient cream to make a very thick paste (left-over egg white may be used instead of the cream). Roll out pastry to about one-eighth-inch thickness, rectangular shape. Cut into three strips. Divide nut filling into three portions and place filling down centre of each strip. Fold over sides of pastry (brush one side with a little egg first before folding over other half). You now have three long rolls of pastry each filled with the nut mixture. Plait rolls very loosely, twist into a ring (side where pastry edges were folded over uppermost) and set in a large buttered and floured cake tin. Cover with a cloth and leave to rise in warm place. Then brush over with egg and bake in hot oven (Regulo 5½), lowering heat to Regulo 4 after about fifteen minutes. Brush with icing sugar dissolved in a little rum while still warm and sprinkle with toasted chopped walnuts or almonds.

SCHNECKEN

Puff pastry made with yeast I (page 172)
1 oz. raisins (washed and dried)
1½ oz. ground walnuts
1½ oz. sugar
1 oz. grated chocolate
1 oz. melted butter
Egg for brushing over pastry

Roll out pastry into a rectangular piece, about a quarter of an inch thick. Mix together dry ingredients and sprinkle over pastry, then sprinkle with melted butter. Roll up as for Swiss roll. Cut into slices about half an inch thick. Place, cut side down, on a buttered and floured baking sheet. (Take the little flap of pastry where it was folded over and put it underneath each piece.) Leave to rise in a warm place, then brush with egg and bake in a hot oven (Regulo 5½–6) until golden brown. Stir a few drops rum into some icing sugar and spread over pastry while still warm but not hot.

CREAM CHEESE PASTRIES
TOPFENGOLATSCHEN

Puff pastry made with yeast I (page 172)
½ lb cream cheese
3 oz. sugar
1 oz. raisins
2 egg yolks or 1 egg
A little cream
Grated lemon rind
Egg for brushing over pastry

Wash and dry raisins. Beat cream cheese with sugar and egg yolks (or egg), stir in sufficient cream to give a thick creamy consistency. Add raisins and grated lemon rind. Roll out pastry to about one-eighth-inch thickness. Cut into squares and place a spoonful of the cream cheese filling in centre of each square. Fold all four corners of each square to middle so that filling is completely encased. Secure with a very small round of pastry on top (use pastry cuttings for this). Place pastries on buttered and floured baking sheet and set to rise in a warm place. When well risen brush with egg and bake in hot oven until golden brown (Regulo 5½). Sprinkle with sugar before serving.

FRUIT LOAVES
FRUECHTENBROT

5½ oz. flour	1 oz. sugar
½ oz. yeast	2 oz. butter or margarine
Pinch salt	Egg for brushing over pastry
1 egg yolk	A few blanched almonds
A little milk	

FILLING:

2 oz. walnuts	2½ oz. biscuit crumbs
1 oz. mixed candied peel	⅛ pint rum
2½ oz. hazel nuts	¼ gill Vanilla liqueur (or
2½ oz. dates (after stoning)	Kirsch)
2½ oz. figs	A little grated orange rind
2½ oz. currants	A little lemon juice
2½ oz. raisins	1 oz. pistachios
5 oz. sugar	2½ oz. almonds (not blanched)

Chop walnuts, pistachios, hazel nuts, dates, figs, almonds and mixed peel. Put in a bowl, add lemon juice, orange rind, raisins, currants, rum and vanilla liqueur (or Kirsch). Cover and leave overnight. On the next day add the sugar and the biscuit crumbs and mix everything together.

Sift flour and salt into a bowl. Dissolve sugar and yeast in about half a cup of tepid milk and add to flour (do not let it 'prove'). Add the egg yolk and the butter (or margarine) cut into small pieces. Knead to a dough. Roll out dough on a floured pastry board as thin as possible. Cut into squares or rectangles. Place a good portion of the filling in centre of each square, fold over pastry and secure edges. Place the small loaves (pastry fold underneath) on a buttered and floured baking sheet, well apart. Brush with egg yolk and leave to dry in a cool place. When egg yolk has dried, brush with egg white and decorate with halved blanched almonds. Place in a pre-heated oven (Regulo 4) and bake until golden brown.

GATEAUX AND ICINGS

*

THERE is no real translation for *Torte*, and for want of a better name I have referred to the recipes in the following chapter as *Gateaux*. That they stand in a group all by themselves no one will dispute. Most significant perhaps is their pristine look, the absence of all superfluous trimmings. No sickly swirls of mock-cream tinted a rich pink, no false pretences—decorations sim ply are not worn. A smoothly rounded top, a modest sprinkling of grated chocolate or nuts, a preserved cherry or two—that is all. Occasionally, though rarely, a tiny swirl of the good filling that goes inside. As if just that much had been left over and couldn't bear to be wasted. . . .

Some *Torten* are filled and iced, others iced only. Sometimes the filling spreads over top and sides of the *gateau* as well, or the top may just be dusted with icing sugar. Never be tempted to have several layers when there is only sufficient filling for one good spread—you should be able to taste the filling, not merely guess at its presence!

If at all possible, have a copper bowl for whisking egg whites. Pre-heat the oven—always. Use a cake tin with a removable bottom so that the cake slides out easily. Cool the cake on a sieve or a rack, upside down. This is important, for the cake should also be iced that way: the absolutely flat part which touched the baking tin uppermost. If the cake has risen too much during the baking, trim it a little so that it stands straight.

KATHI'S SPECIAL ROULADE

Kathi is part of the family. She is my mother-in-law's cook in Vienna and has ruled her with a rod of iron for the last thirty-four years. Her culinary achievements are numerous, but this is my favourite:

½ pint milk (scant)
Pinch of salt and sugar
1 rounded dessertspoon
  butter

2 rounded teaspoons potato
  flour
2 rounded teaspoons flour
4 eggs

Separate egg yolks and whites. Heat the milk with sugar and salt. Melt the butter, stir in potato flour and flour, do not let it brown. Add the hot milk gradually, stirring all the time, cook until thick. Remove from fire, beat in the egg yolks one by one, and when cooled, fold in stiffly beaten egg whites. Spread on buttered and floured paper and bake until golden brown (Regulo 5). Turn on a board sprinkled with icing sugar, remove paper and roll pastry lightly over fresh paper sprinkled with sugar.

CREAM FILLING:
3 egg yolks
1 teaspoon gelatine

2 tablespoons vanilla sugar
A little rum
½ pint cream

Dissolve gelatine in a little water. Whisk egg yolks with sugar over steam until thickened, remove from heat, add the gelatine and whisk until cool, adding a little rum at the same time. Whisk cream until thick, add a little sugar to taste and fold whipped cream into the egg mixture.

Spread thickly over the pastry and fold over very lightly—do not roll up tightly as for Swiss roll. Spread outside of roll with some more sweetened whipped cream and chill before serving. Kathi hands strawberry purée folded into an equal quantity of whipped cream separately. Did I say that she rules us with a sugared rod of iron?

ALPENBUTTERTORTE

This is my favourite birthday cake. I do not know where the recipe originally came from—I only know that it has been with my family ever since my great-grandmother could remember!

CAKE:

2 *eggs*   2½ *oz. icing sugar*

1 *egg yolk*   2 *oz. flour*

CREAM:

½ *cup cream*   2½ *oz. butter*

2 *egg yolks*   2½ *oz. vanilla sugar*

A tiny pinch flour

Place eggs, egg yolk and sugar in a bowl and whisk until very thick and creamy. Fold in sifted flour. Bake in a buttered and floured cake tin at Regulo 4½ for about thirty minutes. Cool on rack or on a sieve, then cut once or twice and fill with the following cream:

BUTTERCREAM FILLING: Place egg yolks, flour and cream in a bowl and whisk over steam until thick. Remove from fire and whisk until cool. Cream butter and sugar and work in the egg cream in teaspoonfuls.

Cover top and sides of *gateau* with melted jam, leave to dry, then spread with thin coffee icing. Decorate with glacé cherries.

BISKOTTENTORTE

Put three ounces hazel nuts or almonds (or a mixture of both) on a baking sheet and toast lightly in oven. Grind, then pour over half a cup of hot milk and leave to cool. Cream three ounces butter with three ounces sugar, gradually work in two egg yolks. Finally add cooled nuts which will by now have become rather mushy. Butter a cake tin. Fill a soup plate with milk, add a few drops rum. Quickly dip some finger biscuits into the milk, taking care that they should not get too wet. Line the cake tin with the sponge fingers, cover with a layer of cream, then with another layer of 'dipped' sponge fingers, a layer of cream, finishing with sponge fingers. Cover with a buttered plate and weigh down. Chill well (overnight if possible, otherwise at least two hours). Slide out cake carefully, cut some sponge fingers to the same height as the *gateau* and stick around the cake, tie with a ribbon. If possible pile a little whipped cream on top of *gateau*, sprinkle with grated chocolate or grated toasted almonds or hazel nuts. Alternatively, keep back some of the cream used for filling, spread smoothly over top and sprinkle with toasted almonds, etc., as before.

MARBLED CREAM SLAB
BUNTER REHRUECKEN

Whisk two eggs with two ounces icing sugar over steam until thick, remove from fire, whisk until cool. Fold in two ounces flour. Line a baking sheet with buttered and floured paper, spread with mixture and bake until pale golden brown (Regulo 5). Remove from baking sheet and take off paper while still warm. Line an oblong buttered cake tin with this pastry, keeping back enough of the pastry to make a 'lid'.

Cream six ounces butter with four ounces icing sugar. Divide into three parts. Colour one part with a few drops pint culinary colouring, add a little Maraschino. Colour second park green, add a few drops rum. Add one ounce melted and cooled chocolate to third part. Spread each layer separately into pastry shell, placing a layer of lightly poached fruit (drained quick-frozen fruit is excellent for this purpose) between each layer of cream. Cover with pastry 'lid'. Chill well. Unmould and spread chocolate icing over top and sides.

CREAM GATEAU
CREMETORTE

4 oz. flour	*2 oz. butter*
3½ oz. icing sugar	*3 eggs*

Separate egg yolks and whites. Keep whites for the filling, also set aside three and a half ounces of the icing sugar. Sift together flour and remaining sugar (one ounce). Make a well in centre, drop in the yolks, crumble butter into flour. Quickly work to a dough and divide into three equal parts. Using a cake tin as a guide, roll pastry into three equal-sized rounds, lay on a buttered baking sheet, prick with a fork and bake separately until light golden brown (Regulo 4). Leave to cool a little, remove carefully from baking sheet. Whisk egg whites until stiff, fold in two ounces icing sugar, whisk until smooth. Fold in remaining sugar. Sandwich together cake rounds with this mixture, set carefully on buttered and floured baking sheet and bake at Regulo ½ until filling has set. Serve dusted with icing sugar.

DOBOS TORTE

This is a truly luscious layer cake where the thickness of the cream filling should equal that of the pastry. The whole thing is decorated with a crisp brown sugar top.

There is no difficulty in preparing the pastry and a kind *patissier* even taught me a little trick for a professional finish which I am only too happy to pass on. The sugar top is a little more difficult—you have to work pretty fast and for the first few times you might find it better to aim at *Dobos Schnitten* (*Dobos* Slices) rather than a *gateau*, as slices are so much easier to cope with.

FOR THE GATEAU: 2½ *oz. icing sugar*
3 *eggs*   2 *oz. flour*

Sift flour twice. Separate egg yolks and whites. Whisk egg yolks with half the sugar until thick. Whip egg whites until stiff, fold in remaining sugar. Fold egg whites into yolks, alternately with the flour. Spread buttered and floured cake

tins of equal size thinly with this mixture and bake in pre-
heated oven until golden brown (Regulo 5 for about fifteen
minutes). Remove carefully from tins and cool. When quite
cold place pastry rounds between sheets of waxed paper, cover
with a board and weigh down (the *patissier's* trick).

For the filling you have the choice of two recipes:

DOBOS FILLING I

2 oz. *butter*	2 oz. *chocolate*
2 oz. *icing sugar*	1 *egg yolk*

Break chocolate into small pieces and melt in warm place.
Cream butter, add melted chocolate and sugar, beat well. Add
egg yolk, continue stirring until cream is light and fluffy.

DOBOS FILLING II:

2 *eggs*	2 oz. *butter*
2 oz. *sugar*	1 oz. *ground toasted hazel*
2 oz. *chocolate*	*nuts*

Break chocolate into small peces and put in a bowl over steam
to soften. When soft, take from fire, stir once or twice, add
sugar and eggs. Return to steam and whip until thick and
creamy. Remove from steam, whisk until cool. Cream butter,
add chocolate cream gradually, finally stir in the toasted hazel
nuts.

Trim pastry rounds and spread with the cream. Set aside
one round for the top on a board very lightly dusted with flour.
Dissolve two and a half ounces sugar in one dessertspoon water
over a low flame, add a small knob of butter and cook until
sugar colours pale golden brown. Remove from fire, cool a
little, then spread quickly over top sheet of pastry. Mark into
slices at once with a knife frequently dipped into hot water.
Replace top on *gateau*, spread a little chocolate cream round
sides.

If sugar top has hardened too quickly, place pastry round

in oven for a few seconds to soften, then mark as described before.

STRAWBERRY GATEAU
ERDBEERKUCHEN

2 oz. *blanched ground almonds*
3 oz. *butter*
3 oz. *sugar*
3 *eggs*
1½ oz. *flour*
1½ oz. *biscuit or cake crumbs*
1 lb. *strawberries (wild straw-berries for preference)*

¼ lb. *icing sugar*
A few drops Maraschino and
   lemon juice
Redcurrant jelly
Glacé fruit
Thin water icing (see
   page 204)

Separate egg yolks and whites. Cream butter and sugar, add the egg yolks. Fold in stiffly beaten egg whites, alternately with the ground almonds, flour and crumbs. Bake in a well-buttered and floured cake tin at Regulo 4½. Remove from tin while still warm, cut once when cold.

Dust the strawberries with icing sugar and pass through a sieve. Add a few drops Maraschino and lemon juice, bind with redcurrant jelly. Fill cake with two-thirds of this purée, pile remaining purée on top of cake. Sprinkle with glacé fruit (chopped) and cover the whole cake with thin white water icing. Alternately you can arrange a layer of halved straw-berries on top of the purée and mix your icing with lemon juice instead of water which gives a pleasant sharp tang.

SEMOLINA CAKE
GRIESS TORTE

3½ oz. *icing sugar*
3 *eggs*
1 oz. *blanched ground almonds*

A little lemon juice and
   grated lemon rind
2 oz. *semolina*

Separate egg yolks and whites. Add lemon juice to yolks and whisk with icing sugar until thick, fold in stiffly beaten egg whites alternately with semolina and ground almonds. Add lemon rind. Bake in a well-buttered and floured cake tin at Regulo 4½. Cover cake with melted jam and thin lemon icing.

HAZEL NUT GATEAU I
HASELNUSSTORTE I

4 *eggs*	1 *oz. melted butter*
2 *oz. ground hazel nuts*	1½ *oz. flour*
2 *oz. icing sugar*	*Whipped cream*

Separate egg yolks and whites. Whisk egg yolks with sugar until thick. Fold in stiffly beaten egg whites alternately with the hazel nuts and the flour, finally add melted butter. Divide mixture and bake in two separate sandwich tins (Regulo 5) until golden brown. Remove from tins while still hot, leave to cool on a rack. Sandwich the two halves together with a generous quantity of sweetened whipped cream into which you have folded one or two tablespoons of toasted, ground hazel nuts.

Top with whipped cream, sprinkle with toasted ground hazel nuts.

HAZEL NUT GATEAU II
HASELNUSSTORTE II

2½ *oz. icing sugar*	2½ *oz. toasted hazel nuts*
4 *eggs*	1½ *oz. breadcrumbs*

FILLING:

⅛ pint milk (scant)   2 egg yolks or 1 egg
2 oz. sugar   ½ teaspoon flour
1 oz. hazel nuts   1½ oz. butter

For the cake, separate egg yolks and whites of three eggs. Whisk egg yolks, whole egg and sugar until thick, fold in stiffly beaten whites alternately with the ground toasted hazel nuts and breadcrumbs. Bake at Regulo 4 for about forty minutes.

When cold cut once or twice and fill either with jam or the following cream: Cook all ingredients except the butter on top of a double-boiler, stirring all the time. Mixture must not boil. Remove when thickened, stir until cool, add to creamed butter. Dust top of *gateau* with icing sugar.

COFFEE CREAM GATEAU I
KAFFEECREMETORTE I

2½ oz. hazel nuts   5 oz. icing sugar
2½ oz. blanched almonds   3 egg whites

CREAM: 4 tablespoons strong black
4 oz. icing sugar   coffee
3 egg yolks   4 oz. butter

Place hazel nuts on a baking sheet and put in hot oven (Regulo 6) for a few minutes. Rub in a tea towel until all the skins come away. Toast almonds lightly in oven. Grind almonds and hazel nuts and mix together. Whisk egg whites until stiff, whisk in half the sugar, fold in remaining sugar lightly. Fold in almonds and hazel nuts. Bake in two separate cake tins until pale golden brown—Regulo 5, about twenty to twenty-five minutes. (This mixture is rather delicate while hot and stiffens quickly as it cools—in order to avoid crumbling or breakage use a cake tin with a removable bottom.) Remove cakes from tins while still hot, leave to cool on a rack. Sandwich together with the following cream, spreading it also over top and sides:

Whisk egg yolks with coffee and sugar over steam until thick. Remove from fire and cool, stirring from time to time. Cream butter and add the egg-cream by the spoonful. Alternately, if real cream is available, use as filling sweetened whipped cream to which a dash of very strong black coffee has been added.

COFFEE CREAM GATEAU II
KAFFEECREMETORTE II

(Made with egg whites only)

3 *egg whites*   3 *oz. icing sugar*
3 *oz. ground blanched almonds* ½ *oz. breadcrumbs*

CREAM:
1 *egg white*   2½ *oz. sugar*
⅛ *pint strong black coffee*

Whisk egg whites, fold in icing sugar and whisk again. Fold in blanched almonds and breadcrumbs. Divide mixture into two equal parts, bake separately (Regulo 5) for about thirty minutes.

When cold sandwich together with the following cream, spreading it also over top and sides of *gateau*. Sprinkle with chopped toasted hazel nuts:

Dissolve sugar in coffee over low flame. Increase heat and bring sugar solution to 240° F. Whisk egg white until stiff. Pour boiling sugar solution over egg white, whisking all the time. Beat until cool.

For a slightly different version brush each cake round on both sides with strong black coffee to which a dash of rum has been added, then sandwich together with cream as above.

CHESTNUT GATEAU I
KASTANIENTORTE I

2½ oz. butter
2½ oz. sugar
3 egg yolks
2 egg whites

CREAM:
2 egg yolks
2 tablespoons cream

3½ oz. cooked sieved chestnuts,
   weighed after sieving,
   passed through a sieve
1 oz. grated chocolate

2 oz. sugar
1½ oz. chocolate
3 oz. butter

Cream butter with sugar, add egg yolks gradually. Stir in grated chocolate, then fold in stiffly whipped egg whites alternately with the chestnuts. Bake in buttered tin at Regulo 4. Leave in cake tin for a little to cool, slide out carefully. For the cream whisk together egg yolks and top milk over steam until thick, remove from fire and whisk until cool. Melt chocolate, cream butter and stir in melted chocolate. (Chocolate must not be hot and should be only just spreadable.) Add egg mixture very gradually. Cut cake once or twice, fill with cream and dust top with icing sugar.

CHESTNUT GATEAU II
KASTANIENTORTE II

2¼ oz. icing sugar
3 eggs
2¼ oz. chestnuts weighed after
   boiling, peeling and sieving
1½ oz. fine breadcrumbs

FILLING:
¼ pint cream
2 oz. chestnuts weighed after
   boiling, peeling and sieving
Sugar to taste

Separate egg yolks and whites. Whisk egg yolks with sugar until thick and pale yellow in colour. Fold in stiffly beaten egg whites alternately with chestnuts and breadcrumbs. Bake at Regulo 4 for about forty minutes.

For the filling whip cream until stiff, fold in chestnuts and a little sugar to taste. Cut cake once and fill with cream, spreading it also over top and sides.

LINZERTORTE

There are many, many versions of this very popular recipe which is a jam tart rather than a *gateau*. You could choose from *Linzertorte weiss* (white *Linzertorte*) made either with blanched almonds or without almonds altogether, or *Linzertorte braun* (brown *Linzertorte*) where almonds or nuts play a prominent part.

Then there is *Linzertorte geruehrt* which means that butter (or margarine) are creamed before the dry ingredients are added rather than crumbling the butter into the dry ingredients. And so it goes on. . . . There is even supposed to be a 'real and genuine' *Linzertorte* originating in the town of Linz (the supposed birthplace of the cake), but rumour has it that this is far, far inferior to all 'copies'!

5 oz. sugar	Pinch powdered cloves and
5 oz. flour	cinnamon
5 oz. butter	2 egg yolks or 1 egg
5 oz. ground almonds (not	Jam for filling
blanched)	Egg for brushing over
Juice of ½ lemon	pastry

Mix together all dry ingredients. Cut butter into small pieces, crumble into dry ingredients, add egg yolks (or egg). Quickly work to a dough, chill for a little. Roll out two-thirds of the pastry, line bottom and sides of a buttered and floured flan case with this. Spread with good jam, arrange a criss-cross pattern over the top with the remaining pastry. Brush over with egg and bake at Regulo 5. When cold dust thickly with icing sugar.

GERUEHRTE LINZERTORTE

6 oz. *butter*
3 oz. *sugar*
1 *egg*
7 oz. *flour*

2 oz. *ground almonds, walnuts*
  or hazel nuts
A little grated lemon rind
Jam

Cream butter and sugar, add egg and continue creaming. Work in flour, almonds, etc., and lemon rind. Spread half of this mixture in a buttered and floured cake tin. Cover with a round of rice paper cut to fit and spread with jam to within three-quarters of an inch of the edge. With the help of a forcing bag pipe the remaining mixture round the edge, also pipe a criss-cross pattern over the jam. Bake at Regulo 4 for about forty-five minutes. Dust with icing sugar when cold.

MERANER TORTE

5 oz. *butter*
5 oz. *icing sugar*
3 *eggs*
5 oz. *ground almonds (not*
  blanched)

2 oz. *grated chocolate*
Pinch cinnamon and powdered
  cloves

Separate egg yolks and whites. Cream butter (or margarine) and sugar, add egg yolks gradually. Fold in stiffly beaten egg whites alternately with the remaining ingredients. Bake at Regulo 4½ for about forty minutes. When cold spread top and sides with hot jam and cover with chocolate icing.

MUERBE TORTE I

6 oz. *butter*
4 oz. *hazel nuts*
4 oz. *sugar*

7 oz. *flour*
1 *teaspoon baking powder*

Sift together flour and baking powder, sift again, then add sugar. Cut butter into small pieces, crumble into flour and sugar. Add hazel nuts and quickly work to a dough. Divide into three equal parts and bake separately (Regulo 5). Fill with cream as for *Nusstorte* (see below) or *Panamatorte* (see page 194). Dust top with icing sugar.

MUERBE TORTE II

5 oz. flour	Rind of ½ lemon
5 oz. butter	2 oz. icing sugar
2 hard-boiled egg yolks	Jam for filling

Sift dry ingredients, cut butter into small pieces and crumble into dry ingredients. Divide dough into two equal portions, roll into rounds and bake separately. When cold sandwich together with jam and dust top thickly with icing sugar. Mashed and sugared raspberries are a good alternative filling to jam.

NUT GATEAU
NUSSTORTE

3 eggs	A little rum
2½ oz. sugar	1 oz. fine breadcrumbs
2½ oz. ground walnuts	

CREAM:	
2 oz. ground walnuts,	3 egg yolks
3 oz. sugar	¼ pint cream
	Dash rum

Separate egg yolks and whites. Whisk yolks with sugar, moisten breadcrumbs with rum. Fold stiffly beaten egg whites into yolks, alternately with walnuts and breadcrumbs. Bake in buttered and floured cake tin (Regulo 4½) for about forty minutes. When cool, cut once or twice and fill with the following cream:

Put cream, sugar and walnuts in a thick saucepan, cook gently until thick. Remove from fire, turn into a bowl and stir until cool. Whisk in egg yolks and rum. Spread top and sides of cake with hot jam, cover with thin lemon or rum icing, decorate with nuts. Halved walnuts, previously dipped in caramel sugar, make a nice decoration.

ORANGE GATEAU
ORANGENTORTE

3 *eggs*	4½ *oz. icing sugar*
Juice and grated rind of	4½ *oz. ground, blanched*
½ *orange*	*almonds*

Separate egg yolks and whites. Whisk egg yolks with three ounces icing sugar to ribbon stage. Add orange juice and whisk again. Whisk egg whites until stiff, add remaining icing sugar and whisk until smooth. Fold egg whites into yolks alternately with ground almonds. Bake at Regulo 4 for about thirty-five minutes. When cold, cover with hot jam, spread orange icing over top. Decorate with orange sections dipped into sugar boiled to 'soft ball' stage.

PANAMATORTE

CAKE:	2 *oz. chocolate*
3 *eggs*	2½ *oz. ground almonds (not*
2½ *oz. icing sugar*	*blanched)*
CREAM:	1 *oz. chocolate*
2½ *oz. butter*	1 *egg*
2½ *oz. sugar*	*About* 1 *oz. toasted almonds*

Grate chocolate and mix with ground almonds. Separate egg yolks and whites. Whisk egg yolks with two ounces sugar until thick and creamy. Whip egg whites until stiff, fold in remaining sugar and whisk again until smooth. Fold egg whites into egg yolks, alternately with chocolate-almond mixture. Bake in buttered and floured cake tin at Regulo 4 for about one hour.

When cold, cut once or twice and fill with the following cream (leaving enough cream to cover top and sides of *gateau*). Break chocolate into small pieces and put in warm place to melt. Cream butter and sugar, add softened chocolate and beat in the egg. Beat mixture really well—it should be quite thick and fluffy. Sprinkle top and sides of *gateau* (after spreading with cream) with toasted and coarsely chopped almonds.

EASTER GATEAU
OSTERTORTE

3 *eggs*

2½ *oz. sugar*

2½ *oz. ground blanched*
    almonds

1½ *oz. flour*

CREAM:

1 *egg*

2 *oz. sugar*

1½ *oz. butter*

1 *oz. chocolate*

Separate egg yolks and whites. Whisk egg yolks with sugar until thick and creamy. Whip egg whites until stiff. Fold beaten egg whites into egg yolks, alternately with ground almonds and flour. Bake at Regulo 4½ in a buttered and floured cake tin for about forty minutes. When cold, cut and fill with the following cream:

Whip egg and sugar over steam until thick. Remove from fire and whisk until cool. Cream butter, add softened chocolate and finally add egg mixture very gradually. Spread top and sides of *gateau* with hot jam, cover with chocolate icing.

WHITSUN GATEAU
PFINGSTTORTE

CAKE:

2½ oz. sugar

2½ oz. blanched almonds,
  ground finely

3 egg yolks

2 egg whites

CREAM:

1 egg white

2½ oz. sugar

⅛ pint water

1 dessertspoon rum

Whisk egg yolks with sugar, fold in stiffly beaten egg whites
alternately with the ground almonds. Bake in buttered and
floured cake tin for about thirty-five minutes (Regulo 4½).
Turn out of tin and cool on a rack.

Prepare filling by dissolving sugar in water over low flame.
Increase heat and cook to 240° F. Whisk egg white until stiff
in a separate bowl while sugar cooks. Pour hot sugar solution
on to stiffly beaten egg white, whisking all the time. Add rum
and whisk until smooth. Cut cake once or twice, fill with this
cream and dust top with sugar.

PISCHINGER TORTE

This consists of special round wafers sandwiched together
with chocolate cream, the recipe for which is given below. In
Austria most of these wafers were manufactured by a firm
called Pischinger—hence the name. The wafers are obtainable
in some Soho shops under the name of *Karlsbader Oblaten.*

2½ oz. chocolate

2 tablespoons water

2½ oz. icing sugar

2 oz. butter

1 egg yolk

2 oz. almonds

Toast almonds lightly in oven, grind. Break chocolate into

small pieces, add water and melt over low flame or over steam. Stir, remove from fire and leave to cool. Cream butter and sugar, stir in yolk and melted chocolate and finally one ounce ground almonds. Spread wafers with this cream and sandwich together. Leave top untouched, but spread cream over sides. Sprinkle sides with remaining ground almonds.

PUNCH GATEAU
PUNSCH TORTE

4 *eggs*	2 *tablespoons rum*
3 *oz. sugar*	*Juice of* 1 *orange*
3 *oz. flour*	⅛ *pint water*
1 *scant oz. butter*	*A few drops Maraschino*
3 *oz. lump sugar*	1 *tablespoon apricot jam*

Whisk eggs and sugar until thick and creamy, fold in sifted flour. Finally stir in melted butter. Bake at Regulo 4 for about forty minutes.

When quite cold cut through twice (the middle layer should be slightly thicker). Spread inside of top and bottom slice with jam. Cut middle layer into small cubes. Rub lump sugar on orange rind, then put sugar, water, rum, Maraschino and orange juice in a saucepan and bring to boil. Pour over the cake cubes, add the jam and mix well. Fill cake with this mixture, press down lightly and glaze with hot jam. Cover top and sides with pink icing.

PAULINENTORTE

My family used to declare with great pride that this recipe was invented by and named after an aunt of mine. As her name really was Paula and, furthermore, as she was very partial to chocolate *gateau*, this may well be true. I have certainly never come across this recipe anywhere else—in fact, the only record I have of it was written in the self-same aunt's own hand-writing. . . .

1 *good oz. ground almonds*	2 *oz. grated chocolate*
(*not blanched*)	*Rind and juice of ½ lemon*
1 *scant oz. breadcrumbs*	2 *oz. icing sugar*
1 *tablespoon rum*	3 *eggs*

Separate egg yolks and whites. Place breadcrumbs in a bowl, moisten with the rum. Sprinkle ground almonds and grated chocolate over the top. Whisk egg yolks with the sugar until thick, add lemon juice and rind. Whip egg whites until stiff, fold into yolks alternately with the other ingredients. Bake for about forty minutes at Regulo 4½. Cover with chocolate icing.

One day, by mistake, I used Maraschino instead of rum for moistening the breadcrumbs. With due apologies to my late aunt (who was a far, far better cook than I can ever hope to be) this was considered a great improvement. . . .

SACHERTORTE

There are a great many myths surrounding the famous *Sacher-torte*. One, that it was invented by the now almost legendary Frau Anna Sacher. This is untrue, for it was the founder of the Sacher dynasty, Franz Sacher, who created it in the days when he was still a chef. Herr Sacher is supposed to have said soon afterwards: 'He bothered me and bothered me to invent something new. As if my *patisserie* were not good enough. So what could I do—I just flung together some ingredients—and there you are.' ('He' was Herr Sacher's employer, Prince Metternich.) Which just goes to show what the 'fling' of a master hand can produce.

Myth number two is that the recipe is a secret held only by the House of Demel. It is quite true that Demel are the sole *concessionnaires* allowed to fix the 'Genuine Sachertorte' seal (in finest chocolate) upon their merchandise, but the recipe itself is no longer secret. It was published in full (with permission of Mr. Eduard Sacher, Jnr.) in *Die Wiener Konditorei* by Hans Skrach (Verlag fuer Jugend und Volk, Vienna), quoting among other ingredients, eighteen egg whites and fourteen egg yolks!

Of course, no self-respecting Viennese housewife will agree that it is the real recipe. Every one of them will assure you that her own version (passed down from grandmother) is the one and only one. I make no such claim . . . though of course my grandmother once told me . . . but we shall not go into that! Now if you were to compare my *Sachertorte* with the one bought at Demel . . .

5 oz. chocolate	*5 oz. icing sugar*
6 eggs	*5 scant oz. flour*
5 oz. butter	

Sift flour twice. Separate egg yolks and whites. Break chocolate into small pieces, add a tablespoon of water and put in a warm place to melt. (Some cooks maintain that rum or Madeira should be used instead of the water and that it should only be added after the chocolate has melted.) Cream butter with four ounces sugar, add egg yolks gradually. Add the melted chocolate (which must be soft but not hot) and stir well. Whisk egg whites until stiff, whisk in remaining 1 oz. sugar. Fold stiffly beaten egg whites into butter/chocolate mixture alternately with the flour. Bake in buttered and floured cake tin at Regulo 4 for about fifty to sixty minutes (cake tin about 9½ inches). When cold spread with warmed apricot jam.

For the CHOCOLATE ICING break four ounces plain chocolate into small pieces, put to melt in oven. Dissolve four ounces sugar in a quarter of a gill of water and cook to 'small thread' stage. Remove from fire and leave to cool. Stir lukewarm sugar solution into melted chocolate, add a drop of good olive oil. Stir constantly until mixture has thickened sufficiently to spread over *gateau*.

Two things should be noted above all others with *Sacher-torte*: the *gateau* should not be very high and the thickness of the icing should about equal that of the apricot jam. It is not true that whipped cream is *always* served with *Sachertorte*, no one in Vienna will heap it on your *Sachertorte* without asking you first whether you like it. It is, however, true that whipped cream is very, very good with *Sachertorte*. . . .

MY OWN METHOD:

I had always been warned that a fate worse than death would befall my *Sachertorte* if I did not follow these instructions implicitly and to the last flick of the egg whisk. Somehow I held a strong distrust for that particular 'old cooks' tale'. Perhaps because I kept remembering Sacher's supposed comment about the 'flinging together' of ingredients. So one day I decided that it was time I had a little culinary fling of my own and this is how I made my *Sachertorte* (ingredients as before):

I broke the chocolate into small pieces, put them in a large fireproof bowl with the water to melt in a warm oven. When the chocolate had softened I added the butter (cut up into smallish pieces) and put the bowl back into the oven for another minute, until the butter was just soft, but not 'oily'. I then retrieved the bowl from the oven, inserted a rotary egg whisk into the mixture and began whisking, adding egg yolks and sugar gradually. I continued whisking until the mixture was light and frothy, then folded in the stiffly beaten egg whites and the flour alternately. The cake was baked as described before. And very good it was too—not to say anything of the time saved in preparation. . . .

CREAM CHEESE GATEAU
TOPFENTORTE

Prepare shortcrust pastry with two ounces sugar, four ounces

butter or margarine and six ounces flour, one egg yolk and a
little grated lemon rind. Line a buttered and floured cake tin
with pastry and bake 'blind'.

Cream half a pound cream cheese with three ounces sugar,
beat in three egg yolks and a little grated lemon rind. Gradually
add three-eighths of a pint of milk, finally fold in three stiffly
beaten egg whites and five ounces flour. Pile into the baked
pastry shell, sprinkle with two ounces washed raisins. Bake
for about one hour (Regulo 3).

CHOCOLATE GATEAU WITH ALMONDS I
SCHOKOLADETORTE MIT MANDELN I

2½ oz. chocolate	3½ oz. butter
5 oz. icing sugar	4 eggs
2½ oz. blanched almonds, finely ground	1½ oz. flour
	A little grated lemon rind

Separate egg yolks and whites. Break chocolate into small
pieces and put in a warm place to melt. Sift together ground
almonds with half the sugar. Cream butter and remaining
sugar, add egg yolks gradually. Whisk egg whites until stiff,
fold into creamed butter alternately with sugar-almonds and
flour. Sprinkle in grated lemon rind. Bake for about forty-five
minutes at Regulo 4½. When cold spread with warmed jam
and cover with chocolate icing.

CHOCOLATE GATEAU WITH ALMONDS II
SCHOKOLADETORTE MIT MANDELN II

3 eggs	2½ oz. grated chocolate
2¼ oz. sugar	2¼ oz. ground almonds

Separate egg yolks and whites. Whisk egg yolks with two
ounces sugar until thick and creamy. Whisk egg whites until
stiff, add remaining sugar and whisk until smooth. Fold egg
whites into yolks, alternately with ground almonds and grated
chocolate. Bake at Regulo 4½ for about thirty-five minutes.
Cover with hot jam and chocolate icing.

TRAUNKIRCHNER TORTE

Bake three rounds of pastry as for *Muerbe Torte* (see page 192).
Sandwich together with the following cream, decorating top
of *gateau* with it as well:

Sieve a quarter of a pound of wild strawberries, stir in four
ounces icing sugar. Add a scant teaspoon powdered gelatine
previously dissolved in a little hot water and fold in a quarter
of a pint of whipped cream.

MORELLA CHERRY GATEAU
WEICHSELCREMETORTE

CAKE:

3 *eggs*	2½ *oz. chocolate*
2½ *oz. melted butter*	2½ *oz. sugar*
	2 *oz. flour*

CREAM:

1 *egg yolk*	1 *oz. chocolate*
3½ *oz. sugar*	1 *teaspoon brandy or rum*
3 *oz. butter*	*Chopped morella cherries*

Grate chocolate and set to melt in warm place. Separate
egg yolks and whites. Whisk together egg yolks with half of
the sugar. Whip egg whites until stiff. Whisk remaining sugar
into egg whites, fold egg whites into yolks. Carefully fold in
flour, finally add melted butter and chocolate which should

be melted but not hot. Bake in buttered and floured cake tin at Regulo 4 for about forty minutes.

For the cream, whisk egg yolk with one ounce sugar over steam until thick. Cream butter with remaining sugar, add egg mixture gradually. Add melted (but not hot) chocolate and rum (or brandy). Divide mixture into two parts. Fold chopped morello cherries into one half. Cut cake in half and spread with this cream, replace top. Spread over top and sides with remaining cream, decorate with stoned morella cherries.

SOFT CHOCOLATE GATEAU
WEICHE SCHOKOLADETORTE

1½ oz. butter
1½ oz. sugar
5 eggs

1½ oz. almonds (not blanched)
2½ oz. chocolate

Separate egg yolks and whites of four eggs. Grate chocolate, grind almonds. Cream butter with one ounce sugar, add egg yolks and egg gradually. Whisk egg whites until stiff, whisk in remaining half ounce sugar. Fold whipped egg whites into butter mixture, alternately with the ground almonds and grated chocolate. Bake in buttered and floured cake tin for about one hour (Regulo 4½). When cool spread with warmed jam and cover with chocolate icing.

WHITE ALMOND CAKE
WEISSE MANDELTORTE

3 egg whites
3 oz. icing sugar

3 oz. blanched almonds, finely ground

Whisk egg whites until stiff, whisk in half the sugar. Fold in remaining sugar alternately with the almonds. Bake in a buttered and floured cake tin for about thirty-five minutes

(Regulo 4). When cold spread with hot jam, cover with lemon water icing.

ZEBRA GATEAU
ZEBRA TORTE

3 *egg yolks*   2 *egg whites*
4 *oz. sugar*   2 *oz. chocolate*
4 *oz. ground blanched almonds*

Whisk egg yolks with sugar, fold in ground almonds and stiffly beaten egg whites. Pour half of this mixture into a buttered floured cake tin. Cover with a round of rice paper which fits exactly. Fold grated chocolate into remaining mixture, spread over mixture in cake tin and bake at Regulo 4 for about forty minutes. When cold, separate two halves carefully, sandwich together with jam and cover with thin lemon water icing.

ICINGS

(For *Chocolate Icing* see *Sachertorte,* page 199)

With the exception of *Dobos Torte,* top and sides of all iced *gateaux* (and most pastries and cakes as well) should be spread with warm jam before the icing is applied. This procedure is called *aprikotieren* in Austria, since the jam is invariably apricot jam, though in fact any smooth jam can be used and I have always found redcurrant jelly excellent for this purpose.

The simplest of all icings is the so-called *Water Icing,* where the water is frequently replaced by lemon juice or rum or coffee. Sieve the icing sugar and add a very little water. Do not stir and leave it to stand for about ten minutes, then stir in the required flavouring (orange juice, lemon juice, liqueur, coffee, rum, etc.), add a little more sugar or liquid to obtain a smooth thick paste, which is then spread over the cake. An even simpler version is to stir the liquid into the sieved sugar—with or without any water added, depending on the strength of the flavour required. It is impossible to give quantities as this is solely a question of the water content in the sugar. This type of icing is best for pastries of all kinds and small cakes, but can be used quite successfully for *gateaux*.

Fondant Icing is a different matter altogether and it is best to make a quantity of *fondant* to store and use as required. For this the sugar has to be cooked to a 'medium blow' stage which is about 235° on the sugar thermometer. To test, dip a small wire loop (I use the rounded end of a skewer) into the hot sugar solution, hold it up, blow on it, and medium-sized bubbles should fly off.

Dissolve one pound lump or granulated sugar in a quarter of a pint of water, together with one teaspoon glucose and one teaspoon vinegar. Brush inside of saucepan with a pastry brush previously dipped into cold water, skim off any impurities which rise to the top. As soon as all the sugar has dissolved, increase the heat and bring solution to boil—do not stir. Test as described before and as soon as the 'medium blow' stage is reached, remove saucepan from fire. Pour sugar on to a marble slab, previously sprinkled with water, sprinkling a little cold water over top of sugar as well. Alternatively, simply sprinkle sugar solution in saucepan with cold water. Leave to cool, then work sugar with a spatula or a spoon until white and firm. Knead a little with the hands until *fondant* becomes pliable. Store in a jar, covered with a damp cloth.

To use fondant: Warm a sufficient quantity of *fondant*, stirring constantly. This is best done in a bowl over steam, as the *fondant* must not get hot. Add required flavouring and, if necessary, a little warm water, or sugar solution.

BY WAY OF A SUMMARY

(*from* Der Phaake *by Josef Weinheber*)

By permission of Hoffmann & Campe Verlag, Hamburg

Ich hab sonst nix, drum hab ich gern
ein gutes Papperl, liebe Herrn:
Zum Gabelfruehstueck goenn ich mir
ein Tellerfleisch, ein Kruegerl Bier,
schieb an und ab ein Gollasch ein,
(kann freilich auch ein Bruckfleisch sein),
ein saftiges Beinfleisch, nicht zu fett,
sonst hat man zu Mittag sein Gfrett.
Dann mach ich—es is eh nicht lang
mehr auf Mittag—mein' Gesundheitsgang,
geh uebern Grabn, den Kohlmarkt aus
ins Michaeler Bierwirtshaus.
Ein Huehnersupperl, tadellos,
ein Beefsteak in Madeirasoss,
ein Schweinspoerkelt, ein Rehragout,
Omletts mit Chamgignon dazu,
hernach ein bisserl Kipfelkoch
und allenfalls ein Torterl noch,
zwei Seidel Goess—zum Trinken mag
ich nicht viel nehmen zu Mittag—
ein Flascherl Gumpolds, nicht zu kalt,
und drei, vier Glaserl Wermuth halt.
Damit ichs recht verdauen kann,
zuend ich mir ein Trabukerl an
und lehn mich z'rueck und schau in d' Hoeh,
bevor ich auf mein' Schwarzen geh.
Wann ich dann heimkomm, will ich Ruh,
weil ich ein Randerl schlafen tu,
damit ich mich, von zwei bis vier,
die Decken ueber, rekreier'.
Zur Jausen geh ich in die Stadt
und schau, wer schoene Stelzen hat,

ein kaltes Ganserl, jung und frisch,
ein Alzerl Kaes, ein Stueckl Fisch,
weil ich so frueh am Nachmittag
nicht schon was Warmes essen mag.
Am Abend, muss ich Ihnen sagn,
ess ich gern leicht, wegn meinen Magn,
Hirn in Aspik, Kalbsfrikassee,
ein kleines Zuengerl mit Pueree,
Faschierts und hin und wieder wohl
zum Selchfleisch Kraut, zum Rumpsteak Kohl,
erst spaeter dann, bein Wein zur Not,
ein nett garniertes Butterbrot.
Glaubn S' nicht, ich koennt ein Fresser wern,
ich hab sonst nix, drum leb ich gern. . . .

. . . Since I've nought else, I can enjoy
My victuals all the more my boy:
Elevenses—I don't deny
Myself some meat and beer, and why,
Occasionally, not include
A Goulash? (*Bruckfleisch* too is good),
And juicy beef, though not too greasy
Lest midday find one feeling queasy.
Then for a stroll, a turn or two,
Across the City Ditch, and through
The Kohlmarkt—that's enough if I'm
To reach the Bierwirtshaus in time.
A chicken soup awaits me there—
A soup beyond reproach—a rare
Prime beefsteak in Madeira sauce,
A Goulash (evergreen resource!)
A savoury ragout of venison
A mushroom omelette, and the benison
Of luscious *Kipfelkoch* to follow,
Then *gateau* . . . and I feel less hollow.
Two pints of beer—I do not ask

A lot to drink at lunch—a flask
Of vintage Gumpolds, not too cold,
And vermouths, three or four all told.
Then, in the cause of good digestion,
A long cigar's the best suggestion.
I lean well back and scan the ceiling,
My coffee comes (and a nice full feeling).
So home—and there I must have peace,
From worldly cares to seek surcease
From two till four, and, stretched my length
Beneath the bedclothes, gather strength.
For tea I saunter into town
And scan the menus up and down
For knuckle end of pork—a dish
I'm partial to—a scrap of fish,
Cold gosling and a bite of cheese.
I'm really quite content with these,
For gourmets rigorously exclude,
So early, any *heating* food.
Dinner's upon us! Now I make
A *light* meal, for my stomach's sake.
Some brains in aspic, fricassée
Of veal, and tongue suffice for me . . .
And meat loaf. . . . Or I might enjoy
Smoked pork and cabbage, or would toy
With rumpsteak and a nice savoy,
And only later, 'pon my soul,
Take with the wine a garnished roll.
And now I think you will see why
Good food admits no other tie:
Because I've nothing else, you see
Life looks uncommon good to me. . . .

(*Translated from the Viennese by John Trench*)

INDEX

The index of German titles with English equivalents in brackets appears in the left column, and the English titles with German equivalents on the right. In cases where no English equivalents are given the recipes appear only in the German index.

SALADS

SAVOURY SAUCES

DUMPLINGS

DESSERTS
INCLUDING SWEET SAUCES

CAKES, PASTRIES AND BISCUITS
I. CAKES AND PASTRIES

II. BUNS AND BISCUITS

GATEAUX AND ICINGS

A CATALOG OF SELECTED

DOVER BOOKS

IN ALL FIELDS OF INTEREST

A CATALOG OF SELECTED DOVER BOOKS IN ALL FIELDS OF INTEREST

100 BEST-LOVED POEMS, Edited by Philip Smith. "The Passionate Shepherd to His Love," "Shall I compare thee to a summer's day?" "Death, be not proud," "The Raven," "The Road Not Taken," plus works by Blake, Wordsworth, Byron, Shelley, Keats, many others. 96pp. 5 3/16 x 8 1/4. 0-486-28553-7

100 SMALL HOUSES OF THE THIRTIES, Brown-Blodgett Company. Exterior photographs and floor plans for 100 charming structures. Illustrations of models accompanied by descriptions of interiors, color schemes, closet space, and other amenities. 200 illustrations. 112pp. 8 3/8 x 11. 0-486-44131-8

1000 TURN-OF-THE-CENTURY HOUSES: With Illustrations and Floor Plans, Herbert C. Chivers. Reproduced from a rare edition, this showcase of homes ranges from cottages and bungalows to sprawling mansions. Each house is meticulously illustrated and accompanied by complete floor plans. 256pp. 9 3/8 x 12 1/4. 0-486-45596-3

101 GREAT AMERICAN POEMS, Edited by The American Poetry & Literacy Project. Rich treasury of verse from the 19th and 20th centuries includes works by Edgar Allan Poe, Robert Frost, Walt Whitman, Langston Hughes, Emily Dickinson, T. S. Eliot, other notables. 96pp. 5 3/16 x 8 1/4. 0-486-40158-8

101 GREAT SAMURAI PRINTS, Utagawa Kuniyoshi. Kuniyoshi was a master of the warrior woodblock print — and these 18th-century illustrations represent the pinnacle of his craft. Full-color portraits of renowned Japanese samurais pulse with movement, passion, and remarkably fine detail. 112pp. 8 3/8 x 11. 0-486-46523-3

ABC OF BALLET, Janet Grosser. Clearly worded, abundantly illustrated little guide defines basic ballet-related terms: arabesque, battement, pas de chat, relevé, sissonne, many others. Pronunciation guide included. Excellent primer. 48pp. 4 3/16 x 5 3/4. 0-486-40871-X

ACCESSORIES OF DRESS: An Illustrated Encyclopedia, Katherine Lester and Bess Viola Oerke. Illustrations of hats, veils, wigs, cravats, shawls, shoes, gloves, and other accessories enhance an engaging commentary that reveals the humor and charm of the many-sided story of accessorized apparel. 644 figures and 59 plates. 608pp. 6 1/8 x 9 1/4. 0-486-43378-1

ADVENTURES OF HUCKLEBERRY FINN, Mark Twain. Join Huck and Jim as their boyhood adventures along the Mississippi River lead them into a world of excitement, danger, and self-discovery. Humorous narrative, lyrical descriptions of the Mississippi valley, and memorable characters. 224pp. 5 3/16 x 8 1/4. 0-486-28061-6

ALICE STARMORE'S BOOK OF FAIR ISLE KNITTING, Alice Starmore. A noted designer from the region of Scotland's Fair Isle explores the history and techniques of this distinctive, stranded-color knitting style and provides copious illustrated instructions for 14 original knitwear designs. 208pp. 8 3/8 x 10 7/8. 0-486-47218-3

Browse over 9,000 books at www.doverpublications.com

ALICE'S ADVENTURES IN WONDERLAND, Lewis Carroll. Beloved classic about a little girl lost in a topsy-turvy land and her encounters with the White Rabbit, March Hare, Mad Hatter, Cheshire Cat, and other delightfully improbable characters. 42 illustrations by Sir John Tenniel. 96pp. 5³⁄₁₆ x 8¼. 0-486-27543-4

AMERICA'S LIGHTHOUSES: An Illustrated History, Francis Ross Holland. Profusely illustrated fact-filled survey of American lighthouses since 1716. Over 200 stations — East, Gulf, and West coasts, Great Lakes, Hawaii, Alaska, Puerto Rico, the Virgin Islands, and the Mississippi and St. Lawrence Rivers. 240pp. 8 x 10¾. 0-486-25576-X

AN ENCYCLOPEDIA OF THE VIOLIN, Alberto Bachmann. Translated by Frederick H. Martens. Introduction by Eugene Ysaye. First published in 1925, this renowned reference remains unsurpassed as a source of essential information, from construction and evolution to repertoire and technique. Includes a glossary and 73 illustrations. 496pp. 6½ x 9¼. 0-486-46618-3

ANIMALS: 1,419 Copyright-Free Illustrations of Mammals, Birds, Fish, Insects, etc., Selected by Jim Harter. Selected for its visual impact and ease of use, this outstanding collection of wood engravings presents over 1,000 species of animals in extremely lifelike poses. Includes mammals, birds, reptiles, amphibians, fish, insects, and other invertebrates. 284pp. 9 x 12. 0-486-23766-4

THE ANNALS, Tacitus. Translated by Alfred John Church and William Jackson Brodribb. This vital chronicle of Imperial Rome, written by the era's great historian, spans A.D. 14-68 and paints incisive psychological portraits of major figures, from Tiberius to Nero. 416pp. 5³⁄₁₆ x 8¼. 0-486-45236-0

ANTIGONE, Sophocles. Filled with passionate speeches and sensitive probing of moral and philosophical issues, this powerful and often-performed Greek drama reveals the grim fate that befalls the children of Oedipus. Footnotes. 64pp. 5³⁄₁₆ x 8 ¼. 0-486-27804-2

ART DECO DECORATIVE PATTERNS IN FULL COLOR, Christian Stoll. Reprinted from a rare 1910 portfolio, 160 sensuous and exotic images depict a breathtaking array of florals, geometrics, and abstracts — all elegant in their stark simplicity. 64pp. 8⅜ x 11. 0-486-44862-2

THE ARTHUR RACKHAM TREASURY: 86 Full-Color Illustrations, Arthur Rackham. Selected and Edited by Jeff A. Menges. A stunning treasury of 86 full-page plates span the famed English artist's career, from *Rip Van Winkle* (1905) to masterworks such as *Undine, A Midsummer Night's Dream,* and *Wind in the Willows* (1939). 96pp. 8⅜ x 11. 0-486-44685-9

THE AUTHENTIC GILBERT & SULLIVAN SONGBOOK, W. S. Gilbert and A. S. Sullivan. The most comprehensive collection available, this songbook includes selections from every one of Gilbert and Sullivan's light operas. Ninety-two numbers are presented uncut and unedited, and in their original keys. 410pp. 9 x 12. 0-486-23482-7

THE AWAKENING, Kate Chopin. First published in 1899, this controversial novel of a New Orleans wife's search for love outside a stifling marriage shocked readers. Today, it remains a first-rate narrative with superb characterization. New introductory Note. 128pp. 5³⁄₁₆ x 8¼. 0-486-27786-0

BASIC DRAWING, Louis Priscilla. Beginning with perspective, this commonsense manual progresses to the figure in movement, light and shade, anatomy, drapery, composition, trees and landscape, and outdoor sketching. Black-and-white illustrations throughout. 128pp. 8⅜ x 11. 0-486-45815-6

Browse over 9,000 books at www.doverpublications.com

THE BATTLES THAT CHANGED HISTORY, Fletcher Pratt. Historian profiles 16 crucial conflicts, ancient to modern, that changed the course of Western civilization. Gripping accounts of battles led by Alexander the Great, Joan of Arc, Ulysses S. Grant, other commanders. 27 maps. 352pp. 5⅜ x 8½.   0-486-41129-X

BEETHOVEN'S LETTERS, Ludwig van Beethoven. Edited by Dr. A. C. Kalischer. Features 457 letters to fellow musicians, friends, greats, patrons, and literary men. Reveals musical thoughts, quirks of personality, insights, and daily events. Includes 15 plates. 410pp. 5⅜ x 8½.   0-486-22769-3

BERNICE BOBS HER HAIR AND OTHER STORIES, F. Scott Fitzgerald. This brilliant anthology includes 6 of Fitzgerald's most popular stories: "The Diamond as Big as the Ritz," the title tale, "The Offshore Pirate," "The Ice Palace," "The Jelly Bean," and "May Day." 176pp. 5⅜ x 8½.   0-486-47049-0

BESLER'S BOOK OF FLOWERS AND PLANTS: 73 Full-Color Plates from Hortus Eystettensis, 1613, Basilius Besler. Here is a selection of magnificent plates from the Hortus Eystettensis, which vividly illustrated and identified the plants, flowers, and trees that thrived in the legendary German garden at Eichstätt. 80pp. 8⅜ x 11.
0-486-46005-3

THE BOOK OF KELLS, Edited by Blanche Cirker. Painstakingly reproduced from a rare facsimile edition, this volume contains full-page decorations, portraits, illustrations, plus a sampling of textual leaves with exquisite calligraphy and ornamentation. 32 full-color illustrations. 32pp. 9⅜ x 12¼.   0-486-24345-1

THE BOOK OF THE CROSSBOW: With an Additional Section on Catapults and Other Siege Engines, Ralph Payne-Gallwey. Fascinating study traces history and use of crossbow as military and sporting weapon, from Middle Ages to modern times. Also covers related weapons: balistas, catapults, Turkish bows, more. Over 240 illustrations. 400pp. 7¼ x 10⅛.   0-486-28720-3

THE BUNGALOW BOOK: Floor Plans and Photos of 112 Houses, 1910, Henry L. Wilson. Here are 112 of the most popular and economic blueprints of the early 20th century — plus an illustration or photograph of each completed house. A wonderful time capsule that still offers a wealth of valuable insights. 160pp. 8⅜ x 11.
0-486-45104-6

THE CALL OF THE WILD, Jack London. A classic novel of adventure, drawn from London's own experiences as a Klondike adventurer, relating the story of a heroic dog caught in the brutal life of the Alaska Gold Rush. Note. 64pp. 5³⁄₁₆ x 8¼.
0-486-26472-6

CANDIDE, Voltaire. Edited by Francois-Marie Arouet. One of the world's great satires since its first publication in 1759. Witty, caustic skewering of romance, science, philosophy, religion, government — nearly all human ideals and institutions. 112pp. 5³⁄₁₆ x 8¼.   0-486-26689-3

CELEBRATED IN THEIR TIME: Photographic Portraits from the George Grantham Bain Collection, Edited by Amy Pastan. With an Introduction by Michael Carlebach. Remarkable portrait gallery features 112 rare images of Albert Einstein, Charlie Chaplin, the Wright Brothers, Henry Ford, and other luminaries from the worlds of politics, art, entertainment, and industry. 128pp. 8⅜ x 11.   0-486-46754-6

CHARIOTS FOR APOLLO: The NASA History of Manned Lunar Spacecraft to 1969, Courtney G. Brooks, James M. Grimwood, and Loyd S. Swenson, Jr. This illustrated history by a trio of experts is the definitive reference on the Apollo spacecraft and lunar modules. It traces the vehicles' design, development, and operation in space. More than 100 photographs and illustrations. 576pp. 6¾ x 9¼. 0-486-46756-2

A CHRISTMAS CAROL, Charles Dickens. This engrossing tale relates Ebenezer Scrooge's ghostly journeys through Christmases past, present, and future and his ultimate transformation from a harsh and grasping old miser to a charitable and compassionate human being. 80pp. 5³⁄₁₆ x 8¼. 0-486-26865-9

COMMON SENSE, Thomas Paine. First published in January of 1776, this highly influential landmark document clearly and persuasively argued for American separation from Great Britain and paved the way for the Declaration of Independence. 64pp. 5³⁄₁₆ x 8¼. 0-486-29602-4

THE COMPLETE SHORT STORIES OF OSCAR WILDE, Oscar Wilde. Complete texts of "The Happy Prince and Other Tales," "A House of Pomegranates," "Lord Arthur Savile's Crime and Other Stories," "Poems in Prose," and "The Portrait of Mr. W. H." 208pp. 5³⁄₁₆ x 8¼. 0-486-45216-6

COMPLETE SONNETS, William Shakespeare. Over 150 exquisite poems deal with love, friendship, the tyranny of time, beauty's evanescence, death, and other themes in language of remarkable power, precision, and beauty. Glossary of archaic terms. 80pp. 5³⁄₁₆ x 8¼. 0-486-26686-9

THE COUNT OF MONTE CRISTO: Abridged Edition, Alexandre Dumas. Falsely accused of treason, Edmond Dantès is imprisoned in the bleak Chateau d'If. After a hair-raising escape, he launches an elaborate plot to extract a bitter revenge against those who betrayed him. 448pp. 5³⁄₁₆ x 8¼. 0-486-45643-9

CRAFTSMAN BUNGALOWS: Designs from the Pacific Northwest, Yoho & Merritt. This reprint of a rare catalog, showcasing the charming simplicity and cozy style of Craftsman bungalows, is filled with photos of completed homes, plus floor plans and estimated costs. An indispensable resource for architects, historians, and illustrators. 112pp. 10 x 7. 0-486-46875-5

CRAFTSMAN BUNGALOWS: 59 Homes from "The Craftsman," Edited by Gustav Stickley. Best and most attractive designs from Arts and Crafts Movement publication — 1903–1916 — includes sketches, photographs of homes, floor plans, descriptive text. 128pp. 8¼ x 11. 0-486-25829-7

CRIME AND PUNISHMENT, Fyodor Dostoyevsky. Translated by Constance Garnett. Supreme masterpiece tells the story of Raskolnikov, a student tormented by his own thoughts after he murders an old woman. Overwhelmed by guilt and terror, he confesses and goes to prison. 480pp. 5³⁄₁₆ x 8¼. 0-486-41587-2

THE DECLARATION OF INDEPENDENCE AND OTHER GREAT DOCUMENTS OF AMERICAN HISTORY: 1775-1865, Edited by John Grafton. Thirteen compelling and influential documents: Henry's "Give Me Liberty or Give Me Death," Declaration of Independence, The Constitution, Washington's First Inaugural Address, The Monroe Doctrine, The Emancipation Proclamation, Gettysburg Address, more. 64pp. 5³⁄₁₆ x 8¼. 0-486-41124-9

THE DESERT AND THE SOWN: Travels in Palestine and Syria, Gertrude Bell. "The female Lawrence of Arabia," Gertrude Bell wrote captivating, perceptive accounts of her travels in the Middle East. This intriguing narrative, accompanied by 160 photos, traces her 1905 sojourn in Lebanon, Syria, and Palestine. 368pp. 5⅜ x 8½. 0-486-46876-3

A DOLL'S HOUSE, Henrik Ibsen. Ibsen's best-known play displays his genius for realistic prose drama. An expression of women's rights, the play climaxes when the central character, Nora, rejects a smothering marriage and life in "a doll's house." 80pp. 5³⁄₁₆ x 8¼. 0-486-27062-9

DOOMED SHIPS: Great Ocean Liner Disasters, William H. Miller, Jr. Nearly 200 photographs, many from private collections, highlight tales of some of the vessels whose pleasure cruises ended in catastrophe: the *Morro Castle, Normandie, Andrea Doria, Europa,* and many others. 128pp. 8⅜ x 11¼. 0-486-45366-9

THE DORÉ BIBLE ILLUSTRATIONS, Gustave Doré. Detailed plates from the Bible: the Creation scenes, Adam and Eve, horrifying visions of the Flood, the battle sequences with their monumental crowds, depictions of the life of Jesus, 241 plates in all. 241pp. 9 x 12. 0-486-23004-X

DRAWING DRAPERY FROM HEAD TO TOE, Cliff Young. Expert guidance on how to draw shirts, pants, skirts, gloves, hats, and coats on the human figure, including folds in relation to the body, pull and crush, action folds, creases, more. Over 200 drawings. 48pp. 8¼ x 11. 0-486-45591-2

DUBLINERS, James Joyce. A fine and accessible introduction to the work of one of the 20th century's most influential writers, this collection features 15 tales, including a masterpiece of the short-story genre, "The Dead." 160pp. 5³⁄₁₆ x 8¼. 0-486-26870-5

EASY-TO-MAKE POP-UPS, Joan Irvine. Illustrated by Barbara Reid. Dozens of wonderful ideas for three-dimensional paper fun — from holiday greeting cards with moving parts to a pop-up menagerie. Easy-to-follow, illustrated instructions for more than 30 projects. 299 black-and-white illustrations. 96pp. 8⅜ x 11. 0-486-44622-0

EASY-TO-MAKE STORYBOOK DOLLS: A "Novel" Approach to Cloth Dollmaking, Sherralyn St. Clair. Favorite fictional characters come alive in this unique dollmaking guide. Includes patterns for Pollyanna, Dorothy from *The Wonderful Wizard of Oz,* Mary of *The Secret Garden,* plus easy-to-follow instructions, 263 black-and-white illustrations, and an 8-page color insert. 112pp. 8¼ x 11. 0-486-47360-0

EINSTEIN'S ESSAYS IN SCIENCE, Albert Einstein. Speeches and essays in accessible, everyday language profile influential physicists such as Niels Bohr and Isaac Newton. They also explore areas of physics to which the author made major contributions. 128pp. 5 x 8. 0-486-47011-3

EL DORADO: Further Adventures of the Scarlet Pimpernel, Baroness Orczy. A popular sequel to *The Scarlet Pimpernel,* this suspenseful story recounts the Pimpernel's attempts to rescue the Dauphin from imprisonment during the French Revolution. An irresistible blend of intrigue, period detail, and vibrant characterizations. 352pp. 5³⁄₁₆ x 8¼. 0-486-44026-5

ELEGANT SMALL HOMES OF THE TWENTIES: 99 Designs from a Competition, Chicago Tribune. Nearly 100 designs for five- and six-room houses feature New England and Southern colonials, Normandy cottages, stately Italianate dwellings, and other fascinating snapshots of American domestic architecture of the 1920s. 112pp. 9 x 12. 0-486-46910-7

THE ELEMENTS OF STYLE: The Original Edition, William Strunk, Jr. This is the book that generations of writers have relied upon for timeless advice on grammar, diction, syntax, and other essentials. In concise terms, it identifies the principal requirements of proper style and common errors. 64pp. 5⅜ x 8½. 0-486-44798-7

THE ELUSIVE PIMPERNEL, Baroness Orczy. Robespierre's revolutionaries find their wicked schemes thwarted by the heroic Pimpernel — Sir Percival Blakeney. In this thrilling sequel, Chauvelin devises a plot to eliminate the Pimpernel and his wife. 272pp. 5³⁄₁₆ x 8¼. 0-486-45464-9

AN ENCYCLOPEDIA OF BATTLES: Accounts of Over 1,560 Battles from 1479 B.C. to the Present, David Eggenberger. Essential details of every major battle in recorded history from the first battle of Megiddo in 1479 B.C. to Grenada in 1984. List of battle maps. 99 illustrations. 544pp. 6½ x 9¼. 0-486-24913-1

ENCYCLOPEDIA OF EMBROIDERY STITCHES, INCLUDING CREWEL, Marion Nichols. Precise explanations and instructions, clearly illustrated, on how to work chain, back, cross, knotted, woven stitches, and many more — 178 in all, including Cable Outline, Whipped Satin, and Eyelet Buttonhole. Over 1400 illustrations. 219pp. 8⅜ x 11¼. 0-486-22929-7

ENTER JEEVES: 15 Early Stories, P. G. Wodehouse. Splendid collection contains first 8 stories featuring Bertie Wooster, the deliciously dim aristocrat and Jeeves, his brainy, imperturbable manservant. Also, the complete Reggie Pepper (Bertie's prototype) series. 288pp. 5⅜ x 8½. 0-486-29717-9

ERIC SLOANE'S AMERICA: Paintings in Oil, Michael Wigley. With a Foreword by Mimi Sloane. Eric Sloane's evocative oils of America's landscape and material culture shimmer with immense historical and nostalgic appeal. This original hardcover collection gathers nearly a hundred of his finest paintings, with subjects ranging from New England to the American Southwest. 128pp. 10⅝ x 9. 0-486-46525-X

ETHAN FROME, Edith Wharton. Classic story of wasted lives, set against a bleak New England background. Superbly delineated characters in a hauntingly grim tale of thwarted love. Considered by many to be Wharton's masterpiece. 96pp. 5³⁄₁₆ x 8 ¼. 0-486-26690-7

THE EVERLASTING MAN, G. K. Chesterton. Chesterton's view of Christianity — as a blend of philosophy and mythology, satisfying intellect and spirit — applies to his brilliant book, which appeals to readers' heads as well as their hearts. 288pp. 5⅜ x 8½. 0-486-46036-3

THE FIELD AND FOREST HANDY BOOK, Daniel Beard. Written by a co-founder of the Boy Scouts, this appealing guide offers illustrated instructions for building kites, birdhouses, boats, igloos, and other fun projects, plus numerous helpful tips for campers. 448pp. 5³⁄₁₆ x 8¼. 0-486-46191-2

FINDING YOUR WAY WITHOUT MAP OR COMPASS, Harold Gatty. Useful, instructive manual shows would-be explorers, hikers, bikers, scouts, sailors, and survivalists how to find their way outdoors by observing animals, weather patterns, shifting sands, and other elements of nature. 288pp. 5⅜ x 8½. 0-486-40613-X

FIRST FRENCH READER: A Beginner's Dual-Language Book, Edited and Translated by Stanley Appelbaum. This anthology introduces 50 legendary writers — Voltaire, Balzac, Baudelaire, Proust, more — through passages from *The Red and the Black*, *Les Misérables*, *Madame Bovary*, and other classics. Original French text plus English translation on facing pages. 240pp. 5⅜ x 8½. 0-486-46178-5

FIRST GERMAN READER: A Beginner's Dual-Language Book, Edited by Harry Steinhauer. Specially chosen for their power to evoke German life and culture, these short, simple readings include poems, stories, essays, and anecdotes by Goethe, Hesse, Heine, Schiller, and others. 224pp. 5⅜ x 8½. 0-486-46179-3

FIRST SPANISH READER: A Beginner's Dual-Language Book, Angel Flores. Delightful stories, other material based on works of Don Juan Manuel, Luis Taboada, Ricardo Palma, other noted writers. Complete faithful English translations on facing pages. Exercises. 176pp. 5⅜ x 8½. 0-486-25810-6

FIVE ACRES AND INDEPENDENCE, Maurice G. Kains. Great back-to-the-land classic explains basics of self-sufficient farming. The one book to get. 95 illustrations. 397pp. 5⅜ x 8½. 0-486-20974-1

FLAGG'S SMALL HOUSES: Their Economic Design and Construction, 1922, Ernest Flagg. Although most famous for his skyscrapers, Flagg was also a proponent of the well-designed single-family dwelling. His classic treatise features innovations that save space, materials, and cost. 526 illustrations. 160pp. 9⅜ x 12¼.
0-486-45197-6

FLATLAND: A Romance of Many Dimensions, Edwin A. Abbott. Classic of science (and mathematical) fiction — charmingly illustrated by the author — describes the adventures of A. Square, a resident of Flatland, in Spaceland (three dimensions), Lineland (one dimension), and Pointland (no dimensions). 96pp. 5³⁄₁₆ x 8¼.
0-486-27263-X

FRANKENSTEIN, Mary Shelley. The story of Victor Frankenstein's monstrous creation and the havoc it caused has enthralled generations of readers and inspired countless writers of horror and suspense. With the author's own 1831 introduction. 176pp. 5³⁄₁₆ x 8¼. 0-486-28211-2

THE GARGOYLE BOOK: 572 Examples from Gothic Architecture, Lester Burbank Bridaham. Dispelling the conventional wisdom that French Gothic architectural flourishes were born of despair or gloom, Bridaham reveals the whimsical nature of these creations and the ingenious artisans who made them. 572 illustrations. 224pp. 8⅜ x 11. 0-486-44754-5

THE GIFT OF THE MAGI AND OTHER SHORT STORIES, O. Henry. Sixteen captivating stories by one of America's most popular storytellers. Included are such classics as "The Gift of the Magi," "The Last Leaf," and "The Ransom of Red Chief." Publisher's Note. 96pp. 5³⁄₁₆ x 8¼. 0-486-27061-0

THE GOETHE TREASURY: Selected Prose and Poetry, Johann Wolfgang von Goethe. Edited, Selected, and with an Introduction by Thomas Mann. In addition to his lyric poetry, Goethe wrote travel sketches, autobiographical studies, essays, letters, and proverbs in rhyme and prose. This collection presents outstanding examples from each genre. 368pp. 5⅜ x 8½. 0-486-44780-4

GREAT EXPECTATIONS, Charles Dickens. Orphaned Pip is apprenticed to the dirty work of the forge but dreams of becoming a gentleman — and one day finds himself in possession of "great expectations." Dickens' finest novel. 400pp. 5³⁄₁₆ x 8¼.
0-486-41586-4

GREAT WRITERS ON THE ART OF FICTION: From Mark Twain to Joyce Carol Oates, Edited by James Daley. An indispensable source of advice and inspiration, this anthology features essays by Henry James, Kate Chopin, Willa Cather, Sinclair Lewis, Jack London, Raymond Chandler, Raymond Carver, Eudora Welty, and Kurt Vonnegut, Jr. 192pp. 5⅜ x 8½. 0-486-45128-3

HAMLET, William Shakespeare. The quintessential Shakespearean tragedy, whose highly charged confrontations and anguished soliloquies probe depths of human feeling rarely sounded in any art. Reprinted from an authoritative British edition complete with illuminating footnotes. 128pp. 5³⁄₁₆ x 8¼. 0-486-27278-8

THE HAUNTED HOUSE, Charles Dickens. A Yuletide gathering in an eerie country retreat provides the backdrop for Dickens and his friends — including Elizabeth Gaskell and Wilkie Collins — who take turns spinning supernatural yarns. 144pp. 5⅜ x 8½. 0-486-46309-5

HEART OF DARKNESS, Joseph Conrad. Dark allegory of a journey up the Congo River and the narrator's encounter with the mysterious Mr. Kurtz. Masterly blend of adventure, character study, psychological penetration. For many, Conrad's finest, most enigmatic story. 80pp. 5³⁄₁₆ x 8¼. 0-486-26464-5

HENSON AT THE NORTH POLE, Matthew A. Henson. This thrilling memoir by the heroic African-American who was Peary's companion through two decades of Arctic exploration recounts a tale of danger, courage, and determination. "Fascinating and exciting." — *Commonweal.* 128pp. 5⅜ x 8½. 0-486-45472-X

HISTORIC COSTUMES AND HOW TO MAKE THEM, Mary Fernald and E. Shenton. Practical, informative guidebook shows how to create everything from short tunics worn by Saxon men in the fifth century to a lady's bustle dress of the late 1800s. 81 illustrations. 176pp. 5⅜ x 8½. 0-486-44906-8

THE HOUND OF THE BASKERVILLES, Arthur Conan Doyle. A deadly curse in the form of a legendary ferocious beast continues to claim its victims from the Baskerville family until Holmes and Watson intervene. Often called the best detective story ever written. 128pp. 5³⁄₁₆ x 8¼. 0-486-28214-7

THE HOUSE BEHIND THE CEDARS, Charles W. Chesnutt. Originally published in 1900, this groundbreaking novel by a distinguished African-American author recounts the drama of a brother and sister who "pass for white" during the dangerous days of Reconstruction. 208pp. 5⅜ x 8½. 0-486-46144-0

THE HUMAN FIGURE IN MOTION, Eadweard Muybridge. The 4,789 photographs in this definitive selection show the human figure — models almost all undraped — engaged in over 160 different types of action: running, climbing stairs, etc. 390pp. 7⅞ x 10⅝. 0-486-20204-6

THE IMPORTANCE OF BEING EARNEST, Oscar Wilde. Wilde's witty and buoyant comedy of manners, filled with some of literature's most famous epigrams, reprinted from an authoritative British edition. Considered Wilde's most perfect work. 64pp. 5³⁄₁₆ x 8¼. 0-486-26478-5

THE INFERNO, Dante Alighieri. Translated and with notes by Henry Wadsworth Longfellow. The first stop on Dante's famous journey from Hell to Purgatory to Paradise, this 14th-century allegorical poem blends vivid and shocking imagery with graceful lyricism. Translated by the beloved 19th-century poet, Henry Wadsworth Longfellow. 256pp. 5³⁄₁₆ x 8¼. 0-486-44288-8

JANE EYRE, Charlotte Brontë. Written in 1847, *Jane Eyre* tells the tale of an orphan girl's progress from the custody of cruel relatives to an oppressive boarding school and its culmination in a troubled career as a governess. 448pp. 5³⁄₁₆ x 8¼.
0-486-42449-9

JAPANESE WOODBLOCK FLOWER PRINTS, Tanigami Kônan. Extraordinary collection of Japanese woodblock prints by a well-known artist features 120 plates in brilliant color. Realistic images from a rare edition include daffodils, tulips, and other familiar and unusual flowers. 128pp. 11 x 8¼. 0-486-46442-3

JEWELRY MAKING AND DESIGN, Augustus F. Rose and Antonio Cirino. Professional secrets of jewelry making are revealed in a thorough, practical guide. Over 200 illustrations. 306pp. 5⅜ x 8½. 0-486-21750-7

JULIUS CAESAR, William Shakespeare. Great tragedy based on Plutarch's account of the lives of Brutus, Julius Caesar and Mark Antony. Evil plotting, ringing oratory, high tragedy with Shakespeare's incomparable insight, dramatic power. Explanatory footnotes. 96pp. 5³⁄₁₆ x 8¼. 0-486-26876-4

Browse over 9,000 books at www.doverpublications.com

THE JUNGLE, Upton Sinclair. 1906 bestseller shockingly reveals intolerable labor practices and working conditions in the Chicago stockyards as it tells the grim story of a Slavic family that emigrates to America full of optimism but soon faces despair. 320pp. 5³⁄₁₆ x 8¼.   0-486-41923-1

THE KINGDOM OF GOD IS WITHIN YOU, Leo Tolstoy. The soul-searching book that inspired Gandhi to embrace the concept of passive resistance, Tolstoy's 1894 polemic clearly outlines a radical, well-reasoned revision of traditional Christian thinking. 352pp. 5³⁄₁₆ x 8¼.   0-486-45138-0

THE LADY OR THE TIGER?: and Other Logic Puzzles, Raymond M. Smullyan. Created by a renowned puzzle master, these whimsically themed challenges involve paradoxes about probability, time, and change; metapuzzles; and self-referentiality. Nineteen chapters advance in difficulty from relatively simple to highly complex. 1982 edition. 240pp. 5⅜ x 8½.   0-486-47027-X

LEAVES OF GRASS: The Original 1855 Edition, Walt Whitman. Whitman's immortal collection includes some of the greatest poems of modern times, including his masterpiece, "Song of Myself." Shattering standard conventions, it stands as an unabashed celebration of body and nature. 128pp. 5³⁄₁₆ x 8¼.   0-486-45676-5

LES MISÉRABLES, Victor Hugo. Translated by Charles E. Wilbour. Abridged by James K. Robinson. A convict's heroic struggle for justice and redemption plays out against a fiery backdrop of the Napoleonic wars. This edition features the excellent original translation and a sensitive abridgment. 304pp. 6⅛ x 9¼.
0-486-45789-3

LILITH: A Romance, George MacDonald. In this novel by the father of fantasy literature, a man travels through time to meet Adam and Eve and to explore humanity's fall from grace and ultimate redemption. 240pp. 5⅜ x 8½.
0-486-46818-6

THE LOST LANGUAGE OF SYMBOLISM, Harold Bayley. This remarkable book reveals the hidden meaning behind familiar images and words, from the origins of Santa Claus to the fleur-de-lys, drawing from mythology, folklore, religious texts, and fairy tales. 1,418 illustrations. 784pp. 5⅜ x 8½.   0-486-44787-1

MACBETH, William Shakespeare. A Scottish nobleman murders the king in order to succeed to the throne. Tortured by his conscience and fearful of discovery, he becomes tangled in a web of treachery and deceit that ultimately spells his doom. 96pp. 5³⁄₁₆ x 8¼.   0-486-27802-6

MAKING AUTHENTIC CRAFTSMAN FURNITURE: Instructions and Plans for 62 Projects, Gustav Stickley. Make authentic reproductions of handsome, functional, durable furniture: tables, chairs, wall cabinets, desks, a hall tree, and more. Construction plans with drawings, schematics, dimensions, and lumber specs reprinted from 1900s *The Craftsman* magazine. 128pp. 8⅛ x 11.   0-486-25000-8

MATHEMATICS FOR THE NONMATHEMATICIAN, Morris Kline. Erudite and entertaining overview follows development of mathematics from ancient Greeks to present. Topics include logic and mathematics, the fundamental concept, differential calculus, probability theory, much more. Exercises and problems. 641pp. 5⅜ x 8½.   0-486-24823-2

MEMOIRS OF AN ARABIAN PRINCESS FROM ZANZIBAR, Emily Ruete. This 19th-century autobiography offers a rare inside look at the society surrounding a sultan's palace. A real-life princess in exile recalls her vanished world of harems, slave trading, and court intrigues. 288pp. 5⅜ x 8½.   0-486-47121-7

THE METAMORPHOSIS AND OTHER STORIES, Franz Kafka. Excellent new English translations of title story (considered by many critics Kafka's most perfect work), plus "The Judgment," "In the Penal Colony," "A Country Doctor," and "A Report to an Academy." Note. 96pp. 5$\frac{3}{16}$ x 8¼. 0-486-29030-1

MICROSCOPIC ART FORMS FROM THE PLANT WORLD, R. Anheisser. From undulating curves to complex geometrics, a world of fascinating images abound in this classic, illustrated survey of microscopic plants. Features 400 detailed illustrations of nature's minute but magnificent handiwork. The accompanying CD-ROM includes all of the images in the book. 128pp. 9 x 9. 0-486-46013-4

A MIDSUMMER NIGHT'S DREAM, William Shakespeare. Among the most popular of Shakespeare's comedies, this enchanting play humorously celebrates the vagaries of love as it focuses upon the intertwined romances of several pairs of lovers. Explanatory footnotes. 80pp. 5$\frac{3}{16}$ x 8¼. 0-486-27067-X

THE MONEY CHANGERS, Upton Sinclair. Originally published in 1908, this cautionary novel from the author of *The Jungle* explores corruption within the American system as a group of power brokers joins forces for personal gain, triggering a crash on Wall Street. 192pp. 5⅜ x 8½. 0-486-46917-4

THE MOST POPULAR HOMES OF THE TWENTIES, William A. Radford. With a New Introduction by Daniel D. Reiff. Based on a rare 1925 catalog, this architectural showcase features floor plans, construction details, and photos of 26 homes, plus articles on entrances, porches, garages, and more. 250 illustrations, 21 color plates. 176pp. 8⅜ x 11. 0-486-47028-8

MY 66 YEARS IN THE BIG LEAGUES, Connie Mack. With a New Introduction by Rich Westcott. A Founding Father of modern baseball, Mack holds the record for most wins — and losses — by a major league manager. Enhanced by 70 photographs, his warmhearted autobiography is populated by many legends of the game. 288pp. 5⅜ x 8½. 0-486-47184-5

NARRATIVE OF THE LIFE OF FREDERICK DOUGLASS, Frederick Douglass. Douglass's graphic depictions of slavery, harrowing escape to freedom, and life as a newspaper editor, eloquent orator, and impassioned abolitionist. 96pp. 5$\frac{3}{16}$ x 8¼. 0-486-28499-9

THE NIGHTLESS CITY: Geisha and Courtesan Life in Old Tokyo, J. E. de Becker. This unsurpassed study from 100 years ago ventured into Tokyo's red-light district to survey geisha and courtesan life and offer meticulous descriptions of training, dress, social hierarchy, and erotic practices. 49 black-and-white illustrations; 2 maps. 496pp. 5⅜ x 8½. 0-486-45563-7

THE ODYSSEY, Homer. Excellent prose translation of ancient epic recounts adventures of the homeward-bound Odysseus. Fantastic cast of gods, giants, cannibals, sirens, other supernatural creatures — true classic of Western literature. 256pp. 5$\frac{3}{16}$ x 8¼. 0-486-40654-7

OEDIPUS REX, Sophocles. Landmark of Western drama concerns the catastrophe that ensues when King Oedipus discovers he has inadvertently killed his father and married his mother. Masterly construction, dramatic irony. Explanatory footnotes. 64pp. 5$\frac{3}{16}$ x 8¼. 0-486-26877-2

ONCE UPON A TIME: The Way America Was, Eric Sloane. Nostalgic text and drawings brim with gentle philosophies and descriptions of how we used to live — self-sufficiently — on the land, in homes, and among the things built by hand. 44 line illustrations. 64pp. 8⅜ x 11. 0-486-44411-2

ONE OF OURS, Willa Cather. The Pulitzer Prize–winning novel about a young Nebraskan looking for something to believe in. Alienated from his parents, rejected by his wife, he finds his destiny on the bloody battlefields of World War I. 352pp. 5³⁄₁₆ x 8¼. 0-486-45599-8

ORIGAMI YOU CAN USE: 27 Practical Projects, Rick Beech. Origami models can be more than decorative, and this unique volume shows how! The 27 practical projects include a CD case, frame, napkin ring, and dish. Easy instructions feature 400 two-color illustrations. 96pp. 8¼ x 11. 0-486-47057-1

OTHELLO, William Shakespeare. Towering tragedy tells the story of a Moorish general who earns the enmity of his ensign Iago when he passes him over for a promotion. Masterly portrait of an archvillain. Explanatory footnotes. 112pp. 5³⁄₁₆ x 8¼.
0-486-29097-2

PARADISE LOST, John Milton. Notes by John A. Himes. First published in 1667, *Paradise Lost* ranks among the greatest of English literature's epic poems. It's a sublime retelling of Adam and Eve's fall from grace and expulsion from Eden. Notes by John A. Himes. 480pp. 5³⁄₁₆ x 8¼. 0-486-44287-X

PASSING, Nella Larsen. Married to a successful physician and prominently ensconced in society, Irene Redfield leads a charmed existence — until a chance encounter with a childhood friend who has been "passing for white." 112pp. 5⅜ x 8½. 0-486-43713-2

PERSPECTIVE DRAWING FOR BEGINNERS, Len A. Doust. Doust carefully explains the roles of lines, boxes, and circles, and shows how visualizing shapes and forms can be used in accurate depictions of perspective. One of the most concise introductions available. 33 illustrations. 64pp. 5⅜ x 8½. 0-486-45149-6

PERSPECTIVE MADE EASY, Ernest R. Norling. Perspective is easy; yet, surprisingly few artists know the simple rules that make it so. Remedy that situation with this simple, step-by-step book, the first devoted entirely to the topic. 256 illustrations. 224pp. 5⅜ x 8½. 0-486-40473-0

THE PICTURE OF DORIAN GRAY, Oscar Wilde. Celebrated novel involves a handsome young Londoner who sinks into a life of depravity. His body retains perfect youth and vigor while his recent portrait reflects the ravages of his crime and sensuality. 176pp. 5³⁄₁₆ x 8¼. 0-486-27807-7

PRIDE AND PREJUDICE, Jane Austen. One of the most universally loved and admired English novels, an effervescent tale of rural romance transformed by Jane Austen's art into a witty, shrewdly observed satire of English country life. 272pp. 5³⁄₁₆ x 8¼.
0-486-28473-5

THE PRINCE, Niccolò Machiavelli. Classic, Renaissance-era guide to acquiring and maintaining political power. Today, nearly 500 years after it was written, this calculating prescription for autocratic rule continues to be much read and studied. 80pp. 5³⁄₁₆ x 8¼. 0-486-27274-5

QUICK SKETCHING, Carl Cheek. A perfect introduction to the technique of "quick sketching." Drawing upon an artist's immediate emotional responses, this is an extremely effective means of capturing the essential form and features of a subject. More than 100 black-and-white illustrations throughout. 48pp. 11 x 8¼.
0-486-46608-6

RANCH LIFE AND THE HUNTING TRAIL, Theodore Roosevelt. Illustrated by Frederic Remington. Beautifully illustrated by Remington, Roosevelt's celebration of the Old West recounts his adventures in the Dakota Badlands of the 1880s, from round-ups to Indian encounters to hunting bighorn sheep. 208pp. 6¼ x 9¼. 0-486-47340-6

THE RED BADGE OF COURAGE, Stephen Crane. Amid the nightmarish chaos of a Civil War battle, a young soldier discovers courage, humility, and, perhaps, wisdom. Uncanny re-creation of actual combat. Enduring landmark of American fiction. 112pp. 5³⁄₁₆ x 8¼. 0-486-26465-3

RELATIVITY SIMPLY EXPLAINED, Martin Gardner. One of the subject's clearest, most entertaining introductions offers lucid explanations of special and general theories of relativity, gravity, and spacetime, models of the universe, and more. 100 illustrations. 224pp. 5⅜ x 8½. 0-486-29315-7

REMBRANDT DRAWINGS: 116 Masterpieces in Original Color, Rembrandt van Rijn. This deluxe hardcover edition features drawings from throughout the Dutch master's prolific career. Informative captions accompany these beautifully reproduced landscapes, biblical vignettes, figure studies, animal sketches, and portraits. 128pp. 8⅜ x 11. 0-486-46149-1

THE ROAD NOT TAKEN AND OTHER POEMS, Robert Frost. A treasury of Frost's most expressive verse. In addition to the title poem: "An Old Man's Winter Night," "In the Home Stretch," "Meeting and Passing," "Putting in the Seed," many more. All complete and unabridged. 64pp. 5³⁄₁₆ x 8¼. 0-486-27550-7

ROMEO AND JULIET, William Shakespeare. Tragic tale of star-crossed lovers, feuding families and timeless passion contains some of Shakespeare's most beautiful and lyrical love poetry. Complete, unabridged text with explanatory footnotes. 96pp. 5³⁄₁₆ x 8¼. 0-486-27557-4

SANDITON AND THE WATSONS: Austen's Unfinished Novels, Jane Austen. Two tantalizing incomplete stories revisit Austen's customary milieu of courtship and venture into new territory, amid guests at a seaside resort. Both are worth reading for pleasure and study. 112pp. 5⅜ x 8½. 0-486-45793-1

THE SCARLET LETTER, Nathaniel Hawthorne. With stark power and emotional depth, Hawthorne's masterpiece explores sin, guilt, and redemption in a story of adultery in the early days of the Massachusetts Colony. 192pp. 5³⁄₁₆ x 8¼.
0-486-28048-9

THE SEASONS OF AMERICA PAST, Eric Sloane. Seventy-five illustrations depict cider mills and presses, sleds, pumps, stump-pulling equipment, plows, and other elements of America's rural heritage. A section of old recipes and household hints adds additional color. 160pp. 8⅜ x 11. 0-486-44220-9

SELECTED CANTERBURY TALES, Geoffrey Chaucer. Delightful collection includes the General Prologue plus three of the most popular tales: "The Knight's Tale," "The Miller's Prologue and Tale," and "The Wife of Bath's Prologue and Tale." In modern English. 144pp. 5³⁄₁₆ x 8¼. 0-486-28241-4

SELECTED POEMS, Emily Dickinson. Over 100 best-known, best-loved poems by one of America's foremost poets, reprinted from authoritative early editions. No comparable edition at this price. Index of first lines. 64pp. 5³⁄₁₆ x 8¼. 0-486-26466-1

SIDDHARTHA, Hermann Hesse. Classic novel that has inspired generations of seekers. Blending Eastern mysticism and psychoanalysis, Hesse presents a strikingly original view of man and culture and the arduous process of self-discovery, reconciliation, harmony, and peace. 112pp. 5³⁄₁₆ x 8¼. 0-486-40653-9

SKETCHING OUTDOORS, Leonard Richmond. This guide offers beginners step-by-step demonstrations of how to depict clouds, trees, buildings, and other outdoor sights. Explanations of a variety of techniques include shading and constructional drawing. 48pp. 11 x 8¼. 0-486-46922-0

SMALL HOUSES OF THE FORTIES: With Illustrations and Floor Plans, Harold E. Group. 56 floor plans and elevations of houses that originally cost less than $15,000 to build. Recommended by financial institutions of the era, they range from Colonials to Cape Cods. 144pp. 8⅜ x 11. 0-486-45598-X

SOME CHINESE GHOSTS, Lafcadio Hearn. Rooted in ancient Chinese legends, these richly atmospheric supernatural tales are recounted by an expert in Oriental lore. Their originality, power, and literary charm will captivate readers of all ages. 96pp. 5⅜ x 8½. 0-486-46306-0

SONGS FOR THE OPEN ROAD: Poems of Travel and Adventure, Edited by The American Poetry & Literacy Project. More than 80 poems by 50 American and British masters celebrate real and metaphorical journeys. Poems by Whitman, Byron, Millay, Sandburg, Langston Hughes, Emily Dickinson, Robert Frost, Shelley, Tennyson, Yeats, many others. Note. 80pp. 5³⁄₁₆ x 8¼. 0-486-40646-6

SPOON RIVER ANTHOLOGY, Edgar Lee Masters. An American poetry classic, in which former citizens of a mythical midwestern town speak touchingly from the grave of the thwarted hopes and dreams of their lives. 144pp. 5³⁄₁₆ x 8¼. 0-486-27275-3

STAR LORE: Myths, Legends, and Facts, William Tyler Olcott. Captivating retellings of the origins and histories of ancient star groups include Pegasus, Ursa Major, Pleiades, signs of the zodiac, and other constellations. "Classic." — *Sky & Telescope.* 58 illustrations. 544pp. 5⅜ x 8½. 0-486-43581-4

THE STRANGE CASE OF DR. JEKYLL AND MR. HYDE, Robert Louis Stevenson. This intriguing novel, both fantasy thriller and moral allegory, depicts the struggle of two opposing personalities — one essentially good, the other evil — for the soul of one man. 64pp. 5³⁄₁₆ x 8¼. 0-486-26688-5

SURVIVAL HANDBOOK: The Official U.S. Army Guide, Department of the Army. This special edition of the Army field manual is geared toward civilians. An essential companion for campers and all lovers of the outdoors, it constitutes the most authoritative wilderness guide. 288pp. 5³⁄₁₆ x 8¼. 0-486-46184-X

A TALE OF TWO CITIES, Charles Dickens. Against the backdrop of the French Revolution, Dickens unfolds his masterpiece of drama, adventure, and romance about a man falsely accused of treason. Excitement and derring-do in the shadow of the guillotine. 304pp. 5³⁄₁₆ x 8¼. 0-486-40651-2

TEN PLAYS, Anton Chekhov. *The Sea Gull, Uncle Vanya, The Three Sisters, The Cherry Orchard,* and *Ivanov,* plus 5 one-act comedies: *The Anniversary, An Unwilling Martyr, The Wedding, The Bear,* and *The Proposal.* 336pp. 5³⁄₁₆ x 8¼. 0-486-46560-8

THE FLYING INN, G. K. Chesterton. Hilarious romp in which pub owner Humphrey Hump and friend take to the road in a donkey cart filled with rum and cheese, inveighing against Prohibition and other "oppressive forms of modernity." 320pp. 5⅜ x 8½. 0-486-41910-X

THIRTY YEARS THAT SHOOK PHYSICS: The Story of Quantum Theory, George Gamow. Lucid, accessible introduction to the influential theory of energy and matter features careful explanations of Dirac's anti-particles, Bohr's model of the atom, and much more. Numerous drawings. 1966 edition. 240pp. 5⅜ x 8½. 0-486-24895-X

TREASURE ISLAND, Robert Louis Stevenson. Classic adventure story of a perilous sea journey, a mutiny led by the infamous Long John Silver, and a lethal scramble for buried treasure — seen through the eyes of cabin boy Jim Hawkins. 160pp. 5³⁄₁₆ x 8¼. 0-486-27559-0

Browse over 9,000 books at www.doverpublications.com

THE TRIAL, Franz Kafka. Translated by David Wyllie. From its gripping first sentence onward, this novel exemplifies the term "Kafkaesque." Its darkly humorous narrative recounts a bank clerk's entrapment in a bureaucratic maze, based on an undisclosed charge. 176pp. 5³⁄₁₆ x 8¼. 0-486-47061-X

THE TURN OF THE SCREW, Henry James. Gripping ghost story by great novelist depicts the sinister transformation of 2 innocent children into flagrant liars and hypocrites. An elegantly told tale of unspoken horror and psychological terror. 96pp. 5³⁄₁₆ x 8¼. 0-486-26684-2

UP FROM SLAVERY, Booker T. Washington. Washington (1856-1915) rose to become the most influential spokesman for African-Americans of his day. In this eloquently written book, he describes events in a remarkable life that began in bondage and culminated in worldwide recognition. 160pp. 5³⁄₁₆ x 8¼. 0-486-28738-6

VICTORIAN HOUSE DESIGNS IN AUTHENTIC FULL COLOR: 75 Plates from the "Scientific American – Architects and Builders Edition," 1885-1894, Edited by Blanche Cirker. Exquisitely detailed, exceptionally handsome designs for an enormous variety of attractive city dwellings, spacious suburban and country homes, charming "cottages" and other structures — all accompanied by perspective views and floor plans. 80pp. 9¼ x 12¼. 0-486-29438-2

VILLETTE, Charlotte Brontë. Acclaimed by Virginia Woolf as "Brontë's finest novel," this moving psychological study features a remarkably modern heroine who abandons her native England for a new life as a schoolteacher in Belgium. 480pp. 5³⁄₁₆ x 8¼. 0-486-45557-2

THE VOYAGE OUT, Virginia Woolf. A moving depiction of the thrills and confusion of youth, Woolf's acclaimed first novel traces a shipboard journey to South America for a captivating exploration of a woman's growing self-awareness. 288pp. 5³⁄₁₆ x 8¼. 0-486-45005-8

WALDEN; OR, LIFE IN THE WOODS, Henry David Thoreau. Accounts of Thoreau's daily life on the shores of Walden Pond outside Concord, Massachusetts, are interwoven with musings on the virtues of self-reliance and individual freedom, on society, government, and other topics. 224pp. 5³⁄₁₆ x 8¼. 0-486-28495-6

WILD PILGRIMAGE: A Novel in Woodcuts, Lynd Ward. Through startling engravings shaded in black and red, Ward wordlessly tells the story of a man trapped in an industrial world, struggling between the grim reality around him and the fantasies his imagination creates. 112pp. 6⅛ x 9¼. 0-486-46583-7

WILLY POGÁNY REDISCOVERED, Willy Pogány. Selected and Edited by Jeff A. Menges. More than 100 color and black-and-white Art Nouveau–style illustrations from fairy tales and adventure stories include scenes from Wagner's "Ring" cycle, The Rime of the Ancient Mariner, Gulliver's Travels, and Faust. 144pp. 8⅜ x 11. 0-486-47046-6

WOOLLY THOUGHTS: Unlock Your Creative Genius with Modular Knitting, Pat Ashforth and Steve Plummer. Here's the revolutionary way to knit — easy, fun, and foolproof! Beginners and experienced knitters need only master a single stitch to create their own designs with patchwork squares. More than 100 illustrations. 128pp. 6½ x 9¼. 0-486-46084-3

WUTHERING HEIGHTS, Emily Brontë. Somber tale of consuming passions and vengeance — played out amid the lonely English moors — recounts the turbulent and tempestuous love story of Cathy and Heathcliff. Poignant and compelling. 256pp. 5³⁄₁₆ x 8¼. 0-486-29256-8

Browse over 9,000 books at www.doverpublications.com